Twisted Roots

Twisted Roots:
Latin America's Living Past

Carlos Alberto Montaner

Translated by Louis Aguilar and Marilú del Toro

Algora Publishing
New York

Library of Congress Cataloging-in-Publication Data

Montaner, Carlos Alberto.
 [Las Raíces Torcidas de América Latina. English]
 Twisted roots : the historical and cultural influences that shaped
Latin America / by Carlos Alberto Montaner.
    p. cm.
Includes bibliographical references and index.
 ISBN 0-87586-261-6 (hard : alk. paper) — ISBN 0-87586-260-8 (pbk. :
alk. paper) — ISBN 0-87586-203-9 (ebook)
 1. Latin America—History. 2. Social conflict—Latin America—History. 3.
Legitimacy of governments—Latin
America—History. I. Title.

 F1410.M717513 2003
 980—dc22

                              2003019568

Printed in the United States

An indispensable book for understanding why Latin America has been, until now, an unfulfilled promise. — Mario Vargas Llosa

Translators' Note:
Quotations were translated from the author's Spanish and were not taken from the original English, in the case that the text had been written in English, or from published English translations of texts written in another language.

The titles that appear in English of publications that were originally written in another language were either already in existence or were a direct translation from a simple title. For other, more difficult titles, they either appear only in the original language or, in the case of Spanish titles, they appear in the original Spanish and my own translation.

The word "liberal" to refer to a political inclination is used to mean favoring little government intervention in the economy.

For Beatriz Bernal, to whom this book and I owe so much

"We live in difficult times during which we can neither speak nor refrain from speaking without running some danger." — Juan Luis Vives (Letter to Erasmus, 1540)

"We are all but heart and soul. Remote from us is the dangerous novelty of thinking."
— University of Cervera ("Declaration of Support to Ferdinand VII," Gaceta de Madrid, May 3, 1827)

"We have before our eyes two great examples: the American Revolution and the French. Let us discreetly imitate the first and carefully avoid the fatal results of the second."
— Francisco de Miranda (1799)

"The only thing to do in America is emigrate."
— Simón Bolívar (1830)

TABLE OF CONTENTS

A Few Words

Why is Latin America the poorest and most underdeveloped region in the West? Let us go straight to the heart of the matter: this book is based on the painful hypothesis that Latin America's patent economic failure, political instability and poor scientific contribution stem greatly from its unique history.

This is a history that, from its inception, has been viewed as corrupt and unjust even by its protagonists — Spaniards, Creoles, Indians, and Blacks. Each group has its own aggrieved perspective and all are partly justified. It's a history that blended the *machismo* of the conquerors with that of the conquered, and to this day it is brutally undermining women, the disadvantaged half of Latin America. It's a history in which the social fabric that emerged, loosely woven from assorted ethnic remnants, never managed to form a state reflecting the interests and values of the immense majority, and a history that inspired certain customs and attitudes along with a specific economic mindset that resisted the creation and preservation of wealth. A history, in short, that failed to foster scientific originality or technical inventiveness, perhaps because the people were never able to overcome the circumscribed educational framework of the culture and the repressive mechanisms that gave rise to a mindset that is resistant to progress.

This book is based on a series of lectures on Latin American identity I gave in 1997 at the Francisco Marroquín University of Guatemala and in the summer of 2000 at the University of Miami as part of a special program directed by historian and political scientist Jaime Suchliki. These talks were open to the public, for I intended to project a historical view of Latin America useful not only to students, but also to any intelligent or merely curious person who has ever asked what was keeping Latin America down.

The eighth chapter, "Escape from the Labyrinth," is based on the last lecture I taught at Lima's Peruvian University of Applied Sciences in the summer of 1999, at the behest of its president, former senator and noted defender of civil liberties Luis Bustamante Belaúnde. The chapter concluded a series entitled, "A Different History of Latin America." This piece, the logical conclusion to my work, responds to the agonizing question derived from my previous argument: if Latin America's historical roots are rotten, is it then condemned to eternal underdevelopment, tyranny, and cultural backwardness? Or, might Latin America some day take its place among the other leaders of Western progress? Fortunately, the answer is hopeful: the 20th century has taught us, especially after World War II, that economic growth is attainable and that poverty and stunted growth are surmountable. Spain, Portugal, South Korea, Singapore and Taiwan demonstrate just that. Chile, today, is also pointing in that promising direction.

What was once conceived as one large piece has become two shorter, more distinct works. This book is the first half. The second book (forthcoming), focuses on the foundations of Ibero-American culture.

I am grateful to these universities and their directors for these academic forums, which led to exciting intellectual interaction. Of course, none of the statements made here is the responsibility of these institutions. They merely provided the stove — I lit the burner and brewed the concoction.

Likewise, I owe a debt of gratitude to Professors Beatriz Bernal, Gastón Fernández de la Torriente, Laura Ymayo and Leonardo Fernández-Marcané for their attentive reading of the manuscript. They pointed out discrepancies and generalizations and made valuable suggestions. I also give thanks to my assistant, Ana Grille, who kindly and patiently organized the index, and to Linda Montaner, my wife, who made intelligent observations throughout the writing of this book.

1. A Suspicious Origin: Fraud, Sophisms, and Other Theological and Judicial Traps

In the first days of the year 2000, a group of Ecuadorian colonels attempted to seize power, repeating a scenario that had been played out a dozen times throughout history in every capital of South America. To paraphrase Marx, it was like the performance of a well-known farce that almost always ended in tragedy.

It often seems as if in that part of the world, democracy — that is, government ruled by laws and elected with the free consent of the majority — is the exception, not the rule. Is there anything more Latin American than the shameful spectacle of pistol-waving soldiers bursting into the presidential palace as government officials flee out the back door? At the close of the 20th century, only one country in the hemisphere, Costa Rica, was exempt from these afflictions, though twice it witnessed the collapse of institutional order. In 1917, General Federico Tinoco staged a coup that lasted two years; and in 1948, chaotic, disputed elections resulted in a revolution marked by armed conflict and executions. Fortunately, the latter episode ended with the constitutional dissolution of the armed forces and the conversion of barracks into schools, a change of which *ticos* (familiar term for Costa Ricans) are rightfully proud.

The notion that Latin America's worst problem is militarism mistakes the symptom for the disease. The real issue lies more truthfully in the fact that many Latin Americans do not recognize the legitimacy of the state. They do not believe in it. They do not see government officials as public servants elected to work for society. They suspect, instead, that the laws are unjust and that judges sentence unfairly, if, in fact, the legal process is undertaken at all. They assume political and bureaucratic corruption to be a given, believing that the most unscrupulous careerists use their positions to "grease palms" to encourage business deals. Although Latin Americans seek to legitimize their constitutions through referendums, they do it mechanically, as if following a ritual stripped of meaning.

Hence, the weak loyalty to public institutions. Strong ethical bonds and a sense of moral obligation are forged with families, friends, and business associates; the state, in the meantime, is perceived as a distant entity — generally hostile, inefficient, and unjust. This attitude may explain why a majority of Peruvians supported Alberto Fujimori's violent shutdown of Congress in 1992 and why, the same year, 65 percent of Venezuelans backed Hugo Chávez's brutal coup attempted against the constitutional government of Carlos Andrés Pérez. It explains the success of "strongmen" of twentieth-century Latin American history: Juan Vicente Gómez, Trujillo, Somoza, Estrada, Carías, Perón, Pérez Jiménez, Batista, and Castro. The 19th century also had its own *caudillos*: Santa Anna, Rodríguez de Francia, Rosas, Porfirio Díaz, and others in a long, redundant list.

It appears that Latin Americans, as a whole, have not been able to create a state with which they feel comfortable, a state they believe to have legitimate power and institutions and government entities that truly work to serve society. How can that be? The roots of the puzzle are old and are worth a closer look, for history may offer perfectly valid solutions to these problems that have persisted into the 21st century and show no sign of disappearing.

THE ORIGINAL ILLEGITIMACY OF POWER

With the arrival of the conquistadors, the wrongly labeled "Indians" felt they were victims of a devastating injustice — as would seem perfectly logical. These were not tribes of "noble savages" living naked in the jungle, but organized groups of millions of human beings — Incas, Chibchas, Mayas, and Aztecs, among others. Most of them were members of complex societies, and they had properties, traditions, dignitaries, established social classes, historical awareness, complicated theologies, science, schools, forms of writing — hieroglyphics that had begun to develop into a phonetic alphabet and the *quipu*, a device of knotted cords used to record events and log objects — and great urban centers, some larger than many European cities. In short, these were peoples with legal institutions — laws, judges — and a subtle cosmic vision that, just as Christianity did for the Europeans, soothed their metaphysical yearnings.

The Indians' sense of violation and dispossession immediately provoked various reactions. Many tried to escape to regions free of the "white men who ruled the thunder." One Indian allowed his fear to take him much farther. Hatuey, a Qisqueyan chief burned at the stake in Cuba because of his opposition to the conquistadors, told the priest who attempted to console him before his death that he would not allow his soul to ascend to heaven if it meant meeting the Spaniards there again.

Legions resisted in battle as long as they could. A substantial number, such as the Antillean Tainos and many Mayas, took their own lives by hanging themselves or swallowing dirt. Though it is hard to believe, it has been said that some swallowed their tongues until they died of asphyxiation. The Indians must have suffered a terrible sense of fear, impotence and defenselessness, which perhaps explains the tendency to blame their disgrace on the malevolent gods of their pantheon. Only the cruelest, most powerful deities could have unleashed such evil. Their poets wrote sorrowful accounts of the desolation brought about by the outsiders' yoke. One anonymous Inca composed these verses of undefined sadness:

> *Mother, when I die, bury me*
> *Here, where we live,*
> *And when you make tortillas,*
> *Weep for me, Mother.*
> *If anyone comes and asks:*
> *Woman, why do you weep?*
> *Just say the kindling is moist*
> *And the smoke causes these tears.*

Not all of the Spaniards were immune to this suffering. Some — and not only religious leaders such as Father Bartolomé de Las Casas, outspoken defender of the Indians — were conquistadors, men of letters as well as arms. *La Araucana*, Alonso de Ercilla Zuñiga's lengthy epic about the conquest of Chile, is full of admiration for the Indians.

However, this sentiment bore an implicit contradiction that soon became apparent. The Creoles (descended from the Spanish) and the Westernized mestizos quickly and without warning began adopting the Indian view: "The Spaniards, without any right, came and took what belonged to *us*." Whether it was a white man directly descended from the conquistadors espousing this view, or a mestizo who no longer knew the language and customs of his ancestors and preserved only a superficial Indian appearance, the result was the same: the violence imparted by the Spanish had branded the state with a sense of illegitimacy that in later generations created a viewpoint bordering on the irrational. One of its most colorful proponents was Venezuela's Francisco de Miranda, the "precursor" of his country's independence. White, liberal, Francophile, and imbued with the spirit of the Enlightenment, Miranda called for the resurrection of an Inca kingdom to replace the decadent Spanish empire in Hispano-America.

Why did Latin Americans adopt this viewpoint of "a conquered people" while Anglo-Saxon Americans did not? Why did the British and Dutch colonists and their descendants in North America believe, without a doubt, in their affiliation with Europe, while Latin Americans, from the very moment of the conquest, questioned their identity? There are several reasons. The first is cultural. The Spanish conquered an enormous territory that included several civilizations, some of which were easily equal to those in Europe. Any Spanish peasant arriving in Cuzco or Tenochtitlán would have been in overwhelming awe of his surroundings. The Spaniards settled into these urban centers to exploit native labor. By force or intimidation, they immediately began subjecting the natives to their customs. It was inevitable, however, that they, in turn, become strongly influenced by the conquered civilization. (The Arabs who controlled half of Spain for seven centuries had been similarly affected. At the Battle of Granada, the Moors and Christians resembled cousins engaged in a family feud rather than enemies.)

None of these factors existed in the lands "purchased" by British and Dutch settlers from "backward" North American Indians. The natives of the North were mostly hunter-gatherers clustered in small tribes without cities, and the majority of them were still ignorant of agriculture. Demography also explains the contrast: the Spaniards numbered barely 20,000-25,000 in the first 70 years, amid a human mass totaling a thousand times that, around 20,000,000-25,000,000. They immediately began populating the new land with mestizos, promiscuously engaging in multiple relations. This "crossing" created emotional bonds between Europeans and natives that extended in two directions: carnal (or sometimes deeper) love for Indian women, and paternal love for mestizo offspring. The Spaniards came both to care for and to identify with their conquered world.

Attempts to discredit the Spanish conquest by contrasting it with English colonization have overlooked several key factors. What would have happened in 1620 if, instead of disembarking at Plymouth Rock on the sparsely populated Massachusetts coast, the Mayflower pilgrims had come upon a city of half a million inhabitants boasting enormous stone temples and spectacular plazas? Or, to bring the analogy up to our times, what would the United States be like today if Sioux, Comanches, and Iroquois now made up half the population, as Indians do in Guatemala or Bolivia? When the British settled into complex societies with large populations and great urban centers, for instance in India, they had to struggle simply to transfer a model of the state and the language. The transitions in the United States, Canada, and Australia were easier because the absence of refined native cultures facilitated a full-scale transfer of British civilization.

All things considered, was the British-Dutch colonization of America more or less compassionate than the Spanish colonization? In truth, they were similar, both involving certain behavior common to most Europeans. Latin America witnessed the action of the conquistadors, who trampled cruelly on the natives. The British and Dutch acted no better, albeit on a lesser scale. The Plymouth settlers, for example, decimated the Pequot tribe in the war of 1636. Also, just as Montesinos, Las Casas, and the Catholic Church in general denounced these abuses in Latin America, certain groups rallied to the natives' defense in North America. The Methodists and the pacifist Quakers, led by Pennsylvania's founder William Penn, sided with the Native Americans. Penn named the city "Philadelphia" (meaning "brotherly love") to promote better relations between the two groups.

JUST TITLES AND UNJUST CONSEQUENCES

In Latin America, the Spanish, Creoles, mestizos, and Indians each addressed the moral problem of the conquest in their own way. Different viewpoints were taken in Spain, as well, namely at the primary universities where a great theological debate was taking place. This development was crucial in an era and a nation that had made religion the subject of its weightiest reflections and concerns.

Theologians and lawmakers drafted seven *Títulos Justos*, titles establishing the rights of the Spanish Crown, that were articulated in a sort of grand syllogism to legitimize the conquest of America and the new state they had forced on the Indians. The first title states that the emperor is "lord of the world" and therefore of the infidels. The second explains the origin of the emperor's powers, bestowed on him by the pope, who demands in return the Christianization of the infidels. The third, based on natural law and Roman tradition, states that what belongs to no one should become the property of whoever discovers or occupies it. America did not belong to a Christian ruler prior to Spanish-Portuguese arrival; ergo, it should belong to the one who governs these nations by the grace of God. The fourth title returns to religious ground: the infidel or pagan who refuses to accept Christian faith may be subdued by force, subjugated, and enslaved, if necessary.

How, indeed, would the Indian be persuaded to embrace Christianity and surrender to the Spanish Crown? By virtue of *The Requirement*, a legal document magistrate Palacios Rubios wrote in Spanish asserting the supremacy of Christianity and defying the Indians to attack it. First used in 1514, the text was proclaimed in empty hamlets from which its inhabitants had fled, or read to stupefied natives who did not understand a word. If the conquered natives did not accept the new authority, the invaders brandished it as legal-theological sanction to coerce the Indians into submission. It is worthwhile to review a few paragraphs of this incredible document, its translation modernized for easier comprehension:

I require you to ... recognize the Church as the lady and mistress of the entire world; and the Supreme Pontiff, known as the Pope, in her name; and the king and queen, our lords in her stead, masters, lords and rulers of these islands and firm land, by virtue of the given word; and you will consent and give way to what the religious fathers shall declare and preach ... If you do not do this ... with God's help, I shall move forcefully against you and wage war in all areas and forms ... and I will take your persons and your women and children and I shall make slaves of them, and, as such, I shall sell and dispose of them as His Highness commands, and I shall take your goods, as well, and inflict on you all the ills and harm that I can, like vassals who disobey or refuse to receive their lord ... The deaths and wounds ... will be your fault, and not that of his Highness, nor mine, nor of these gentlemen who came here with me; and what I say and require I ask that the present legal clerk give me as signed testament, and beg those present to be witnesses.

The fifth of the *Títulos Justos* addresses the customs and behavior of the "infidels." To subdue a pagan people, it was enough that their conduct offend Christians. Cannibalism, human sacrifice, sodomy, and excessive consumption of alcohol were the gravest outrages. Had God not destroyed Sodom for its perversity? This argument inspired the questionable allegations of sodomy that the conquistadors constantly leveled at the Indians. Whether they engaged in homosexual acts or not, it was convenient to believe they did.

The sixth title addresses the natives' peaceful acceptance of their domination. Paralyzed by fear, many Indians accepted *The Requirement*. Others formed alliances with the Spanish against a third, common enemy, and willingly accepted the yoke.

The seventh title returned to religious reasoning, but now with a fatalistic spin: it was God's will that Spain rule over these territories and their infidels.

But was it so simple? Several religious thinkers, led by the Dominican Francisco de Vitoria and his disciple, Domingo de Soto, drafted arguments against these legitimizing concepts. In the process, these thinkers established the basis for international law.

Francisco de Vitoria is believed to have been born in Burgos a few years before the discovery of America (the date and place are uncertain). At a very young age he went off to Paris, where he entered a Dominican monastery. After he returned to Spain as a doctor of theology, Vitoria was awarded a chair in 1526 at the University of Salamanca, then the country's most prestigious institution next to the University of Alcalá de Henares. Soon, he revolutionized theological studies and teaching methods, putting into practice his extensive French education. A decade after his arrival in Salamanca, he turned his attention to the Indian question and developed his view on the conquest from a theological and legal perspective. He died in 1546.

To Vitoria and to Domingo de Soto, Spain could legitimately govern the Indians if it had their free consent. However, despite the fact that they were infidels, Indians had rights and could not be enslaved for being unfamiliar with Catholicism, a religion they had never before encountered. In any case, what mattered most about Vitoria's reasoning — apart from the fact that it was a theoretical debate with few concrete results in America, except perhaps to influence legislation concerning the Indians — was that it diminished the role of theology in the legitimization of the conquest, emphasizing instead natural law and *jus gentium*. Thus, while the Spanish justified their dominion in the New World by the *Títulos Justos*, they did not stop at the concepts usually referenced in the Judeo-Christian tradition. More limited and humane claims, founded in reason and greater tolerance, were invoked.

Las Casas Against Sepúlveda

Vitoria's work had quite an influence in the academic world of Europe but never quite penetrated Spanish debate on America. The same cannot be said of the horrified accounts of religious leaders who participated in the colonization and witnessed the conquistadors' abuses. The first to sound the alarm — in a sermon appropriately titled *Una voz que clama en el desierto* ("A Cry in the Desert") — was Dominican friar Antonio de Montesinos, in Hispaniola (today Santo Domingo). Shortly before Christmas, in 1511, Montesinos issued a harsh admonishment to a congregation of Spaniards, among them the governor, Diego Colon: "This voice says that all of you are in a state of mortal sin, in which you will live and die, for the cruelty and tyranny you employ against these innocent persons." Montesinos discredited the entire conquest outright:

> With what right and what justice do you maintain these Indians in such cruel and horrible servitude? With what authority have you waged such detestable wars against these people, who were tame and peaceful on their

lands? ... How can you keep them so oppressed and fatigued, without giving them food to eat or curing them of their illnesses, which they incur with excessive labor and from which they die — or shall I say, you kill them to extract and acquire gold every day?

There was a thunderous and two-fold reaction against Montesinos. The local authorities confronted him. Perceiving a threat to their interests, the few hundred Spaniards on the island (there could not have been many in 1511) reported him to King Ferdinand. The most virulent opposition, however, came from Montesinos's own congregation and his immediate superior, Fray Alonso de Loaysa. The friar argued that such words questioning the monarchs' right to their territories, bequeathed by His Holiness the Pope, could only have been put in his mouth by the devil. Still, Montesinos's words were not lost on everyone. One young Andalusian in the church that day, Bartolomé de Las Casas, experienced a revelation.

King Ferdinand reprimanded Montesinos; but he also summoned a council of lawyers and theologians in Burgos to examine the issues in greater depth. From these meetings emerged several recommendations that essentially reiterated the *Títulos Justos* but also proposed a more humane treatment of the Indians, declaring them free beings and, therefore, subjects of the law. Later, in 1512, these principles served as the basis for the Laws of Burgos, a set of provisions designed to "Christianize" and "Spaniardize" the Indians, forcing them to live in villages specially created for them — once their original homes had been destroyed — and imposing on the colonists a labor code that both regulated and mitigated their harsh treatment of the natives.

Because it was the Church's duty to ensure that the laws were obeyed, four years later, in 1516, three Jeromian friars (sending Dominicans would have only added fuel to the fire) set sail for Hispaniola. They arrived with the new legal code in hand and the authority to implement and enforce it. Joining them on the same expedition was the extraordinary and fiery polemicist Las Casas, who was returning to America determined to fight for justice.

Born in 1474, Bartolomé de Las Casas was a Sevillian adventurer who watched his father and uncles sail off with Columbus on the Genoese's second voyage to America in 1493. Four years later, Las Casas enlisted in a punitive operation against a Moorish uprising in Granada. He experienced a religious calling that he successfully combined with his love for the military. In 1502, Las Casas received "minor orders" from the Church, possibly at the level of *lector*, and immediately left for Hispaniola in the company of Nicolás de Ovando, occupying the dual role of soldier and *doctrinero*, or lay teacher of catechism. Five years later, in Rome, he was ordained; he returned to America as cleric and commander, charged with converting the Indians and obtaining their obedience. The Indians were forced to work in brutal conditions in what was really a veiled form of slavery.

Las Casas had been present the day Montesinos made the contradiction clear, and it changed his life. From that moment on, he took up the cause of fighting for decent treatment of the Indians. The battle would unfold over several decades through intrigues and political maneuverings, nonetheless including lofty debates and a serious intellectual effort to harmonize the propagation of faith with the rights of Indians and the alleged rights of the Crown. Engaging in and developing this polemic destabilized the state and shook a source of authority that was, in the eyes of many Americans, Spaniards, Creoles, mestizos, and, of course, Indians, morally contradictory and worthy of censure.

Thus arose a contentious debate between Andalusians — for Las Casas' greatest opponent was the Cordovan lawyer and theologian Juan Ginés de Sepúlveda (of a younger generation, born in 1490), who never set foot on American soil. Sepúlveda's ideas about the conquest and the Indians were purely intellectual constructions. However, his background in the humanities was considerably more extensive than that of Las Casas. He was fluent in Greek and Latin and had an excellent Artistotelian-Thomistic education. Such was the prestige of his erudition that he was appointed chronicler to Emperor Charles V and tutor to the future king, Philip II. His fame as a philosopher — or what today would be called an "ideologue" — stemmed from two works he wrote contradicting Las Casas, *Democrates Primus* and *Democrates Secundus,* or *Concerning the Just Cause of the War Against the Indians.*

Democrates Secundus precipitated the confrontation between the two men. In this work, citing Aristotelian ideas, Sepúlveda adds a new element to the dispute over the "just causes" for subjugating the Indians: their inherently inferior culture. Aristotle suggested the existence of people who were "natural-born slaves," individuals whose innate inferiority fated them to serve superior masters. They were born for this purpose, and there was nothing wrong in using them the way things and animals were used to benefit those occupying a higher plane in the hierarchy of life. Indians, according to Sepúlveda, dwelled on a lower plane, and not strictly due to biological constraints — he did not consider them animals devoid of souls — but for cultural ones manifested in their savage behavioral acts: human sacrifice, bestiality, pederasty, and idolatry. Christian duty called for them to be redeemed from such barbarity, even at the cost of a war of blood and fire — a war sanctioned by the Church's mandate.

Las Casas could not remain silent and allow Sepúlveda's claims to go unchallenged. A lawyer and theologian so close to the emperor and prince could jeopardize the lobbying effort he and others like him had carried out on behalf of the Indians. In 1542 — although it would not be published for another decade — Las Casas wrote the influential tract, *A Brief Report on the Destruction of the Indians.* The document served to promote the New Laws, a set of guidelines adopted that same year favoring the Indians and thereby endangering the system of Spanish estates. A year later, Las Casas was named bishop of Chiapas, a diocese in southern Mexico. In a stormy confrontation there, he excommunicated several landowners. The colonists, fearing the loss of what was practically slave labor at their disposal, made grave accusations against the Dominican. As the landowners verged on insubordination, Viceroy Antonio de Mendoza suspended the New Laws, thus staving off an imminent civil war such as had taken place in Peru over the same legislation.

Las Casas now realized that the struggle had to take place as much in Spain, the seat of power, as in America, where the consequences were felt. Las Casas resigned his bishop's post and returned to his homeland. There, he crossed paths with Sepúlveda, which inspired him to write a pamphlet titled *Apología*. He also called on the Christian conscience of both Charles V and his son, Philip, urging the monarchy to convene a council of experts to examine the war they had waged for the conquest, the conquest itself as an end, and Spanish treatment of the Indians.

The emperor agreed. In the summer of 1550, the finest thinkers of the realm gathered in Valladolid to hear and discuss the arguments put forth by the two religious leaders. It was more than a theoretical colloquium — they would debate the very moral grounds for Spain's presence in the New World and the ways in which it had undertaken the conquest and colonization. Their positions cannot be summarized here, but it is likely that Las Casas, having spent half of his life among the Indians, proved more convincing. Surely he was more eloquent, speaking for a total of five days, while Sepúlveda exhausted his arguments in three hours. At the event's end, the scribe, Domingo de Soto, presented a summary of the arguments to the emperor. He enumerated both sides' points, but his own opinions leaned more toward Las Casas' moral stance than toward Sepúlveda's legalistic, nationalistic rationale. From that moment on, the former bishop of Chiapas officially became defender of the Indians and Sepúlveda, spokesman for the conquistadors and colonists.

The famous debate had another salient consequence. Las Casas took advantage of his testimony before the council to publish soon afterward his *Brief Report on the Destruction of the Indians*, later printed in English as *The Tears of the Indians*. The passionately written pamphlet almost immediately prompted Spain's powerful enemies, England, Holland, and France, to create what has since been called the "black legend," a thoroughly negative description of the ways in which Spain had gained power in the Americas and sought to keep its dubious authority. The work was widely known and read in the New World, where it fueled the resentment of many citizens against the state. Moreover, it fed the belief that the state that was imposed on the continent suffered from almost complete illegitimacy. The impression was spread that the conquest had imposed great cruelty on the Indians, contradicting Christian principles and even the standards dictated by Spain.

The debate between the two men is key to understanding Latin America. Both Bartolomé de Las Casas and Juan Ginés de Sepúlveda were profoundly religious and Spanish — the latter a nationalistic patriot at odds with Dominican beliefs, the former a religious zealot who later supported the Inquisition.

In a way, their extreme faith heightened the permanent tension that existed between Church and state, two institutions inextricably linked in sixteenth-century Spain that would remain so almost to the end of Spanish rule in the first quarter of the 19th century. For the Indians, Las Casas represented the compassionate and protective side of the Church, which they came to cherish as the only institution capable of comforting them in their tragedy. Sepúlveda (although he surely did not realize it) came to personify the state forged through violence. He was the viceroy, the constable, and the landowner — the iron fist. Las Casas and those who stood with him, were the sanctuary. This might explain the apparent paradox of Christian Indians who revered a Church imported and imposed by the Spanish yet rejected the state that oppressed them.

It may also explain the intense religious devotion of Latin American societies with large Indian and mestizo populations, such as those in Mexico, Peru, Guatemala, and Bolivia. When the Mexicans began their war of independence in the 19th century, they called on the Virgin of Guadalupe, giving the impression that she was for them no longer Spain's Virgin, but Mexico's. The supportive attitude of certain clergy had made the Church and Christianity part of Latin American identity. The state, on the other hand, remained a distant and remote entity. In their own way, without discarding certain pre-Columbian customs and beliefs, the Indians became profoundly, radically Christian but never quite converted politically. The state remained foreign, and when the time came, they waged war against Spain, but not against Christianity.

ARISTOTLE IN AMERICA

How did a pagan Greek philosopher born five centuries before Christ become the authority invoked by Spanish Christians in the 16th century to justify conquest and war?

In the twelfth century, first in Oxford and then in Paris, the period's most audacious intelligentsia, led by a pair of Franciscan friars, argued that science and religion existed on two different planes. Science centered on truth observed and proven by reason; religion, on revelation and authoritative testimony. To a 21st century scholar, this distinction seems obvious but to a medieval thinker, it was a terrifying concept. It seemed to impose new boundaries on what had been the Church's exclusive territory. It constituted a giant step toward the secularization of society. Specifically for the Church, it meant that scientific opinions had to be substantiated with rational explanations. The Church could no longer seek refuge in its own authority or the affirmations of its sacred texts.

In the same century, an Arab born in 1126 in Córdoba when it was still Islamic territory, Ibn Rushd, philosopher, lawyer and judge later known as Averroës, rediscovered Aristotle. He translated the Greek into Arabic and retrieved the fundamental idea that reason could unlock the secrets of nature. Society and laws fulfill their ends when they are harmoniously adapted to nature rather than fighting it; and, authority should emanate from society, tempered by rational decisions. This describes the ascending theory of power, which is a pillar of modern democracy. One did not rule by the grace of God — the descending theory of power — but by popular consent. Legitimate power *rose* from the citizens to the top. In 1198, Averroës died in exile in Marrakech of the Almohad Empire, having upset the Church and, in addition, orthodox Muslims who were disturbed by his reinterpretation of the Koran. But, by then, another of his works, *The Incoherence of the Incoherence*, had been translated into Latin. Scholars at the University of Paris, the intellectual center of Christendom, discussed not only Averroës but also Aristotle, newly restored to his pedestal.

This development posed an enormous threat to the Church's authority. Pope Gregory IX forbade professors and students to discuss Aristotle at the University of Paris and appointed two Dominicans of high intellectual repute, the Flemish William of Moerbeke and the German Albertus Magnus, who enlisted his young Italian disciple Thomas Aquinas, to formulate the Church's position on the matter. Of the three, Aquinas did most to perform the assigned task. However, he neither disgraced Averroës, whom he admired, nor refuted Aristotle. Instead, he exalted Aristotle, turning the Greek's vast body of work into the theoretical foundation of Catholicism for a great many centuries to come.

Saint Thomas intended to Christianize Aristotle but accomplished the reverse: he Aristotelianized Christianity. He transformed the philosopher's ideas into the glue that would hold together orthodox Catholicism. If conventional authority, based on revelation, no longer served to judge thoughts and deeds, then Aristotle's reflections, filtered through Aquinas, would become the canon of Catholic orthodoxy. Aristotle's reasoning would become the Church's. The result was a step forward, creating a more tolerant intellectual atmosphere — but not one without dangers. For instance, Aristotle posited that Earth was the center of the universe and the sun orbited around it. Copernicus proved the opposite in the 16th century, and citing the supposedly infallible Aristotle, religious leaders censured him. When Galileo restated the claim in the next century, the Inquisition forced him to recant. Aristotle could not be so easily discounted.

Thomas Aquinas left behind the *Summa theologiae*, a vast work written in Latin, for which he was appointed Doctor of the Church in the 16th century. He died in 1274 at age 48, no doubt partly owing to his obesity. Almost a century after his birth, in 1324, Pope John XXII had Aquinas canonized.

Aristotle and Aquinas were "democrats" in the modern sense of the term: they were proponents of the ascending theory of power. Both believed that citizens as free beings had certain inalienable and natural rights. Both supported limiting the power of royalty through fair laws. Ironically, men like Sepúlveda cited their work to justify warring against and even enslaving the Indians. Granted, coming from a society in which slaves and *metecos* (foreigners without rights) outnumbered free individuals, Aristotle had written that barbarians could be captured and forced to work. By nature, they were not persons, but things. Saint Thomas never corrected or contradicted him. There were no abolitionists in the thirteenth century.

WHAT OF THE CHURCH'S TÍTULOS JUSTOS?

Up until this point, Church endorsement had given Spain moral and legal validation. But, where did the Church get its legitimacy to authorize powers, dispense favors, name princes, and decide the destiny of millions of human beings in America who had never heard of it, or Christ, or Rome?

Spain's and Portugal's "rights" to the New World were established by several papal bulls, dispensed by Pope Alexander VI and reinforced by the 1494 Treaty of Tordesillas between Spain and Portugal. The pope's gracious donation, however, was questioned immediately and rejected summarily by other nations and was not even understood by the wronged natives of the New World. The pope's decision had not been a groundbreaking development, for previous pontiffs had already set the precedent. Adrian IV gave Ireland to the English in the middle of the twelfth century, and Clement VI ceded the Canary Islands to Spain in the fourteenth. Generous donations by Pope Martin V and Pope Eugenius IV in the fifteenth century entitled Portugal to vast African lands. They were pagan territory, so the pontiffs could turn them over to nations willing to convert the inhabitants and, indeed, authorized these nations to enslave and dispossess the natives. Nicholas V must have followed a similar line of reasoning in 1545 when he authorized Portugal's Alfonso V to conquer a large part of Africa's west coast.

One question immediately leaps out at the modern scholar: where did the pope get the authority to distribute global territory? The answer is fascinating, for it springs from a quotation of just a few words in the New Testament when a resurrected Jesus tells his disciples, "Go, and teach all people." These words inspired two apocryphal documents that in large measure were used to decide the course of Western civilization for over a thousand years: the *Epistola Clementis*, a fifth-century fraud hatched by Pope Leo I and purportedly given by Saint Peter to his successors, and the *Donation of Constantine*, another false document from the eighth century, personally presented by Pope Stephen II to Pepin III to confer legitimacy on Pepin as king of the Franks.

This complex series of falsifications began when Roman emperor Constantine adopted Christianity at the beginning of the fourth century. He came not as a believer but, in fact, as just another political power in the Church, presiding over councils and naming or dismissing dignitaries. This led to a delicate struggle between the political and ecclesiastic hierarchies that lasted until the latter half of the 19th century when the pope lost sovereignty over the Papal States and became a moral authority exclusively.

Because of its ties to imperial Roman traditions, Catholic liturgy developed a sacred atmosphere that preserved various pagan symbols. The pope came to be revered much like an emperor, sitting on a throne with a canopy overhead, his subjects genuflecting, and choruses singing hymns. Emperor Constantine and his successors acted like popes; later popes acted like emperors. In Byzantium, in the eastern sector of the Roman Empire, the emperor commemorated the death of Christ with a symbolic Last Supper, attended by 12 members of the aristocracy — one for each Apostle and each Tribe of Israel — where he washed the feet of 12 indigents. The emperor, who used to be the head of the pagan faith, would now lead Catholicism (at least until the bishop of Rome could disentangle himself from the encumbrances of his power structure, a move which ultimately would divide the Church).

Because this marriage between church and state first took place in Constantinople, Catholicism's first centuries were fundamentally Greek, even after supremacy to the bishop of Rome had been acknowledged. How did Rome eventually attain that position of privilege? A passage carefully extracted from the Bible and cleverly promoted served the purpose. According to the gospel of Matthew (16:19), Jesus gave Peter an extraordinary power to act in terrestrial matters, telling him that "whatever you bind on earth will be bound in heaven, and whatever you loose on earth will be loosed in heaven." The passage dispelled any doubt as to whether Peter was the first among the Apostles. He was more than that. He was a sort of vicar of Christ, empowered by the Nazarene to act in His name because the decisions he took would be upheld in heaven.

Still, Matthew wrote nothing of Peter's successors. Where, then, did subsequent occupants of the throne of Peter derive their authority? Halfway through the fourth century, during a struggle between Pope Leo I and secular powers, a letter written by Saint Peter to Pope Clement I appeared, according to accounts, bequeathing Peter's semi-divine gifts to the bishop of Rome, and by extension, the pope. Ironically, the Romans executed Peter in the year 65 or 67, and after his death there were two more bishops of Rome, Linus from 67 to 76 and Anacletus from 76 to 78. The Church eventually canonized both. It seems logical that if Peter had decided to pass his supernatural powers on to a successor, he would have transferred them directly to Linus and not Clement. In any event, among these gifts were the powers to validate rulers and organize the Church by his standards. The pope obeyed no one and could not be judged by his subjects. Only God could hold him accountable. The institution he led was vertical, and power descended from a higher source. The pope wielded it, but God granted it. God was the *pantocrat*, the omnipotent. He had made the pope the *autocrat*, independent of any other power, and the *cosmocrat*, lord and governor of the world.

The pope could therefore legitimize monarchs. In the Bible, the prophets of Israel anointed its kings, and the pope was also a kind of biblical prophet. He could enthrone monarchs. For this end, he used a symbolic crown and sword. The crown signified the authority he bestowed, the sword, the monarch's duty to defend the Church. This is where we get the phrase, still used unto this day, "king by the grace of

God." Only the pope could decide to whom God's grace was granted, for he was God's representative in this vale of tears. Whoever thus assumed authority was responsible for his actions only before God.

Gradually, the pope, also the bishop of Rome, distanced himself from the authority of the emperor in Constantinople. Language became a growing barrier. The Byzantine Greeks lost their command of Latin and the Romans of their Greek. The Bible was translated from Greek into Latin, which in the fifth century, especially, was quickly becoming the primary language of Catholicism. The pope was not overly concerned about this state of deteriorating communication. He was most interested in consolidating his power over Western Europe and evading Byzantine hegemony. He must have suspected that these conflicts would finally result in a schism. Admittedly, Western Europe was a more backward and unruly region, and the barbarians — the Germanic tribes — had destroyed the Western Roman Empire. For Catholic Rome, this was an opportunity more than a problem. The Roman Church would fill the void that was left in the wake of the collapsed political power. The barbarians would be Latinized, not Hellenized. The Christianity they adopted would be Roman and not Byzantine — although, early on, the simpler variation, Arianism (advanced by Bishop Arrio of Alexandria), held sway. With great audacity, the pope ordered Irish missionaries to conquer the world for the glory of the "Roman" Catholic Church. This distinction was highlighted in every document and prayer, and it was a discreet way of emphasizing "anti-Greek."

In the middle of the eighth century, two parallel events occurred that had an enormous impact on history. In the heart of the powerful kingdom of the Franks — encompassing a large portion of what today is France, the Low Countries, and Germany — Pepin the Short, son of Charles Martel and father of Charlemagne, deposed King Childeric III. Meanwhile, further south, another Germanic people, the Lombards, who had penetrated into Italy in the sixth century, threatened to seize the territories of the Church. Pepin ruled the most powerful kingdom in Western Europe, but he was an illegitimate leader and needed some way of validating his authority. Pope Stephen II, for his part, was in danger, and neither could nor would turn to Constantinople for help. Challenging his supremacy in Christendom and his control over lands in Italy, the Byzantine Empire had become a natural enemy.

The Pope traveled to the land of the Franks to extend a *quid pro quo* offer to Pepin: he would legitimize his *de facto* government in return for defending Rome against the Lombards. He took with him the *Donation of Constantine* (today preserved in Paris) — a decisive document and a falsification through and through. Based on an old legend, the document claimed that Constantine, the first Roman emperor to convert to Christianity, knelt at the feet of Pope Sylvester like a *strator* (a servant who walks his master's horse) in gratitude for having been cured of leprosy (a disease he never really had). He transferred all his powers to the pope, giving him his spear, scepter, purple cloak, tunic, and crown. Instead of donning the crown, however, Sylvester returned it to Constantine. He was then the one to name Constantine emperor. As a gift, Constantine donated to the pope all of Italy, which later dwindled down to Ravenna and the Duchy of Rome.

Pepin accepted the pact, and became the defender of Catholicism. The Pope declared Pepin's dynasty lawful. Pepin freed Rome from the ever-menacing specter of the Byzantine Empire, and he ousted the Lombards from the exarchate of Ravenna and other cities and ceded them to the pope, thus laying the foundation of the Papal States. Suddenly, without anyone realizing it, the world's cultural axis had shifted.

Did Pepin suspect that the *Donation of Constantine* was counterfeit? It made no difference, since it was convenient for him to accept it as genuine. From that moment, the emperor ruling Constantinople became nothing more than a Greek king, from which Rome could sever all ties. Thus originated the temporal power of the Supreme Pontiff over the Papal States, territories that remained permanently under papal sovereignty until as late as 1870. A glorious vestige of these territories survives today, its ceilings and walls magnificently painted by Michelangelo: the Vatican.

There were two other colossal consequences. From a political and cultural standpoint, Europe had been born, and the center of its civilization had begun the shift from the Mediterranean to the continent's north. The pope also had acquired the power to legalize monarchs. In the descending theory of power, all power comes from God, as Saint Paul affirmed, and the pope is the first conduit. The pope delegates to the Christian princes the power given to him by God to govern the world. He has become emperor of the world by two means (both apocryphal): his succession to Peter as head of the Church, according to the false *Epistola Clementis*, and Constantine's gesture in the equally fraudulent *Donation of Constantine*.

Europe, then, is born of these falsehoods, and Rome begins to dream of restoring the empire. It cannot be Latin, however. A Germanic people had saved Catholicism. The new entity is called the Holy Roman Empire, although it never truly consolidates. Nonetheless, the pope gains immense political power, so much so that 700 years after the meeting between Pepin and Pope Stephen II, the Spanish, now in America, continue to be subject to that authority and refer to it to validate their actions. Out of this power structure emerged the debatable *Títulos Justos*, which never persuaded Latin Americans completely.

2. One State to the Dissatisfaction of All

The state's original sin in Latin America was not solely of a moral or metaphysical nature. True, there was a sense of spiritual unease, for the conquest was not ethically justifiable and priests and moralists denounced it. A population was robbed of its gods, required to accept alien customs, and forced into brutal labor despite laws and norms recommending better treatment; of course, they rejected the state. However, the native peoples were not the only ones who felt aggrieved. The colonists also resented their treatment by the Spanish Crown.

In effect, three groups participated in the de-legitimization of the state: the Spanish, the Indians and, when there were enough of them, the mestizos. The grievances of the latter two groups, persecuted, profoundly humiliated and offended, are easily understood. But, why did the Spanish feel wronged? There was a fundamental discrepancy between the interests of the conquistadors and the Crown. For the Pizarros, Corteses, and Almagros, the adventure they had undertaken was a matter of private business, and it had been presented to them as such. It was essentially a quest for gold, spices, plunder, slaves, women, and servants that later grew to include vast farms, haciendas, and villas. The conquistadors carried out their intentions. They went into Indian villages and sacked them. They organized cavalry raids — predatory incursions against adversaries who usually were completely helpless. Such plundering was ethically acceptable in Europe. Why should the Spanish in America hold

27

back, after Charles V's own infuriated military pillaged Rome in 1527 when the emperor could not pay their salaries? A worse massacre occurred in Antwerp in 1576 for similar reasons; Philip II's army slaughtered 8,000 people and destroyed hundreds of buildings.

The quest for glory may have played a part, but most of them were in it for the money. What the conquistadors all had in common was a scant inheritance and a weak financial position back home. They crossed the Atlantic in search of riches that they hoped to take back to Spain. Generally, they were second sons, under the age of 30, better educated than the average man but with no fortune to speak of. The truly wealthy, the great nobles, rarely went to the New World. To "do America," as it was later known, held no appeal for them.

In addition to the taxes that the Crown was quick to impose on the natives and on commercial transactions, the discovery and colonization meant power and authority over a vast, immeasurably large territory, one that grew with each expedition through dense jungles, up mighty rivers, and over lofty mountain ranges. It was also about a land rich in precious metals, which the Spanish quickly came to rely on as a nearly magical way to expand their public treasury, failing to realize that riches thus obtained could one day become a poisoned gift.

THE FIRST "ARMY"

The agreement between the Crown and the colonists, at least in the last decade of the fifteenth century and the first few of the sixteenth, in some ways resembled a *Carta de Mercedes*, or a kind of concession of royal privileges in case discoveries were, in fact, made. In other ways, it resembled what today could be called a joint venture. The conquistadors contributed funds and human capital, that is, brains and manpower. The Crown granted legitimacy and authority, as well as protection against encroaching European powers. The Crown reaped most of the benefits — the monarchs reserved for themselves at least the customary "royal fifth" — but certain important privileges also went to the conquistadors. For instance, through the *Capitulations of Santa Fe*, Christopher Columbus became Viceroy, Governor General, and Admiral of the Oceans, a hereditary title — that Ferdinand the Catholic nevertheless dissolved afterward. (Diego Columbus, the Genoese navigator's son, later governed as viceroy of Hispaniola for some time.)

The *Capitulations* stipulated the relations between the conquistadors and the monarchs and were used to recruit men for the *hueste de conquista*, a kind of "conquering corps" of adventurous mercenaries who voluntarily enlisted together with a captain and negotiated their portion of booty and share of privileges. They generally received no salary, paid for their own arms, and when they had them, supplied their own horses. These private soldiers, who rarely had any real war experience, soon enough clashed with the royal corps, soldiers hired and paid by the public treasury to defend the Crown's interests (and not necessarily those of the conquistadors).

For Columbus' second voyage, the Spanish monarchs — impressed by his first results and the presence in Barcelona of a half-dozen frightened Indians and several parrots of amazing colors — supplied the expedition with 20 mounted lancers from the *Hermandad del Reino de Granada* ("Brotherhood of the Kingdom of Granada"), serving as functionaries for the Spanish state. Ostensibly, they were sent along to assist with the conquest. It seems likely that their more important, covert function was to display the royal standard and securely establish royal authority over Columbus' own, illustrating who was the sovereign and who the vassal.

Curiously, the differences between the *huestes de conquista* and the official army replicated some of the differences that were beginning to distinguish modern times from medieval. The *huestes de conquista* had no regular troops, did not train for combat, and depended on no source of sustenance other than what it could obtain from its own campaigns. Relations between leader and subordinates were not rigidly delineated, although certain factors were taken into account in distributing booty, such as conduct in battle and financial investment in the company. They were more like armed fighting bands than armies, and after a victory they would revert to the life of farmers, ranchers, miners, or bureaucrats. The military institutions of feudalism operated in a similar fashion, except that those marching across America were volunteers.

The *huestes reales*, or official army, followed in the tradition of the Roman military, the mother of all armed forces. The men trained, lived in barracks, and subscribed to an ancient code of honor that condemned cowardice while encouraging aggression, loyalty in battle, and obedience to superior officers. They had, or were expected to have, an *esprit de corps*: a special tribal bond, a gregarious unifying spirit that differentiated them from all other men. They felt, or at least they were intended to feel, unique. Their salute distinguished them: the hand thrust in a certain direction, the heels clicking, the chest lifted. They also counted on visual symbols to reinforce these bonds — uniforms, banners, and insignias — and auditory symbols such as crisp speech, drumbeats, special musical rhythms, whistles, and coronets. They displayed an amazing physical bearing. They moved rapidly, in unison, steps locked, separated at equal distances. They marched, and the cadence of their precise steps, practiced since the defensive Roman formations, resembled a war dance; it provoked an animated state of excitement known as "martial." According to some experts, for reasons science has not yet proved but which may be connected to neurological activity, this state enhances discipline and ferocity in combat, two very convenient factors for annihilating enemies and intimidating observers.

Those who trickled into America were no different. Guards in the service of viceroys and important dignitaries arrived first. More complex military units were sent when pirates, corsairs, and enemy naval powers belonging to England, France, and Holland began attacking coastal cities such as Panama, Veracruz, Cartagena of the Indies, Havana, and San Juan of Puerto Rico. Another dozen urban centers were fortified and armed with fixed and mobile artillery, both of which were unnecessary and excessive to subdue the natives. Such militarism began to take root as a consequence of external dangers. It kept foreign forces away as well as subtly intimidated the colonists. This intimidation may have left an imprint on Latin America. In any case, with the passing of time, military units recruited white Creole troops as well as "dark" and "colored," or mestizo troops. The higher ranks, however, remained Spanish.

As may be expected, it was not long before the Crown and the conquistadors were at odds with each other. Columbus himself wound up in Spain, imprisoned and charged with corruption, abuse, and nepotism, probably as the result of a power struggle. As the *huestes de conquista* advanced through America, royal officials and priests (who generally answered to the monarchs) established the limits of Spanish authority. Every voyage of discovery sent an "entry official" with the conquistadors to protect the riches of the Crown, the monarchs' royal fifth, which was needed to save Spain from its perpetual state of near-bankruptcy resulting from incessant wars.

The conflicts (the struggle between Columbus and his persecutor Commander Francisco de Bobadilla is a dramatic example) began as early as the period of the Catholic monarchs, ending with the death of Ferdinand the Catholic (1516). They continued intermittently during the reigns of Charles I of Spain and V of Germany (1517-1556) and his son, Philip II (1556-1598), the founders of the Hapsburg dynasty. Despite the many nuances of these confrontations, they could be summarized in one melancholy phrase penned by Francisco de Pizarro, conqueror of Peru and himself a protagonist of bloody power struggles: "While I conquered the land and traveled, knapsack on my back, I was never given aid. Now that I have conquered and won it, they send me stepfathers." At different times, Christopher Columbus, Hernán Cortés, and Diego de Almagro felt the same frustration. The Crown prohibited them from exploiting the Indians at will, limited their political decision-making, frequently denied them social distinction, and haggled with them over money matters. The conflict of interests was obvious and constant. Finally, the Spanish state, after stifling a dozen or so conspiracies and bloody revolts — one settled with the killing of Peru's viceroy by angry compatriots — tightened its fist until it won the total subjugation and obedience of both the Indians and the conquistadors.

This control grew more rigid as years passed and it hardened significantly when the Bourbons arrived. Historian of the period J.M. Ots

Capdequí has classified this era as "the reconquest" of America, and so it was. On the heels of the first adventurers came the bureaucrats and their institutions. The fiction sustained by the Crown as well as jurists and theologians until 1519 consisted in portraying America not as a colony, but as a province of the Spanish empire, a legal status probably meant to reaffirm Spanish authority before other European powers rather than benefit the conquistadors and Indians. By the same token, the Indians were not slaves, but citizens in their own right — a very useful distinction designed to tax them as well as protect them from the greed and cruelty of some conquistadors. The reality, however, was otherwise. Indians and mestizos were second- and third-class citizens. As for the captive blacks brought in to replace the exhausted native work force, they had no rights at all.

The Spanish were determined not to interact socially with the Indians — excluding, of course, sexual relations with the women. Within the fiction of the *Reino de Indias*, or the "Kingdom of the Indies," the Spanish created entities they called "republics of the Indians," which consisted of *reducciones*, or villages constructed to accommodate the Indians, with access to only a handful of Spanish officers, doctrinarian priests, and magistrates. One clear objective of these townships was to facilitate their transculturation — teaching the Indians to comport themselves like Spaniards (without, of course, allowing integration). A Jew or Moor who converted to Christianity could, with great difficulty, integrate into Spanish society. An Indian or mestizo always remained on the outside. These towns were also intended to protect the Indians from the cruelty, lechery, and scrupulousness of many conquistadors and colonizers. This noble, segregationist preoccupation led to what today would be call apartheid.

How could so few Spanish command the obedience of thousands of Indians? How could they intern them in those villages and force them to live like Spaniards? There was only one way: by making models of the more prominent Indians, the chiefs and their families. Instead of crushing the old Indian hierarchy — except the most outstanding leaders, who were killed in battle — the Spanish turned the hierarchy into an instrument of their own ruling class. They awarded the Indian chiefs privileges similar to those given to the Spanish to win their loyalty: schools to educate their children, lands, good housing, and, in a few cases, control over less fortunate Indians. A great number of them were allowed to own black slaves.

Out of this arrangement grew a small Indian sub-aristocracy parallel to Spain's but totally in its service. The members of this aristocracy taxed the other Indians — the Spaniards were exempt — bore arms, maintained order, and acted as administrators of local townships. These were the only Indians who, for a long period of time, were permitted to ride horses — animals that were feared and admired by the natives and that were also a status symbol representing the maximum power. Naturally, the hatred of the majority of the native population knew no bounds, but now part of it was reserved for its own people. This hatred cost lives in sporadic uprisings all over the colonial landscape: Jacinto Canek in Yucatan, Tupac Amaru in Peru, and Tupac Catari in Bolivia. Two and a half centuries after the arrival of Columbus, the overwhelming majority of natives could not speak Spanish. They still dreamed in their own languages and in those languages, conjured up impossible rebellions.

If, for Spain, the recently discovered territories were hard to absorb, let alone understand, the opposite was also true in America. From the American perspective, Spain was a remote, alien world. The Spanish on the Iberian Peninsula, like all Western European peoples, felt bound by their king and religion, the only patriotism possible in this era and for three centuries to come. Nationalism, in the modern sense of the word, did not exist. How could one expect the Indians, mestizos, or even the Creoles born in the New World to have the same emotional bond with Spain? How could one hope for the same from Spaniards who felt defrauded by a motherland that barred their advancement despite their merits and personal sacrifices? Spain was a head so distant and different from the body it sought to rule that true synthesis never occurred. It was not a state born of the needs of its citizens, Spanish or otherwise, but merely an instrument of the Crown.

Spain, where the monarchs crushed the conspiracies of rebellious nobles, squashed nationalistic outbreaks, persecuted religious deviations, and expelled different ethnicities (Jews, Moors, and even Christianized Moors), guarded its American possessions like a prize. It viewed any form of autonomy as dangerous, any demand for self-government as suspect. This intense control explains the frustration of the Spaniards transplanted to America. They had pulled off an amazing achievement and were among the most courageous and intelligent conquerors known in history. They had survived untold adversity and danger — without, of course, sparing the conquered. Yet, they were unable to become masters of their own political and economic destinies in the land they had won. Theirs was the feat, but the monarchs took the glory and the lion's share of the spoils.

THE KING, HIS MINISTERS, AND THE LAW

The period between the discovery in 1492 and the beginning of the end of Spanish rule in America in 1808 — marked by the invasion of French troops in Spain — saw three royal families, each tinged with its own personality.

The Catholic monarchy ended with the deaths of Isabella in 1504 and Ferdinand in 1516. The Hapsburgs then took power, beginning with the former Charles V but ending abruptly in 1700 after Charles II (called "the Mad" in English and *el Hechizado* in Spanish because of his weak and inert nature) left no heir. The Bourbons, who rule to this day, then followed; but only after the long, violent War of Succession (1701-1714). This conflict could well be called "global," judging by the varying origins of the participants, the different settings in which it unfolded, and the great number of casualties (1.25 million). It persisted for years, interrupted by the First Republic (1869-1874) and the Second Republic (1931-1939), finally ending after the Civil War.

Originally the Catholic kings and, after Ferdinand's death, the brilliant regent Cardinal Cisneros governed the American territories with the help of the Council of Castile, a sort of ministerial body made up of aristocrats and illustrious figures who advised the monarch. In 1524, however, as the colonization of America grew more complex, the Council of the Indies became the government's supreme organ for the Indian Monarchy erected in 1519. The latter entity was theoretically bound to the Empire of Charles V, along with Castile, Aragon, Naples, and the Low Countries, otherwise known as the Frankish County. This lopsided federation of different nations and territories, supposedly united under one sovereign, in a way signified a much higher degree of self-government for the New World. In practice, it remained a colony firmly directed from the peninsula, even though many local leaders had been born in the Americas.

As for the Council of the Indies, essentially it governed America in the name of the king. It passed legislation, appointed leaders to their posts or threw them out, served as judge and appeals court, punished, rewarded, assigned and revoked privileges, and created legal-political entities — that is, it combined, added, and subtracted territories. In short, it dictated an incredible number of laws and norms. These were the *Leyes de Indias*, or "Laws of the Indies." When for practical reasons they could not be applied, distressed American officials could only ask that they be "observed, but not honored." It was not a matter of disobedience, but of impossibility. No one, states a legal principle born of common sense, is obliged to do the impossible.

Was this huge bureaucratic task of legislation a great work of government, as some thought? Yes, and no. For more than three centuries, it managed the enormous American territory surprisingly well. This long period was peaceful. However, the undeniable benefits were the result of a centralized, statist tradition that encouraged neither individual responsibility nor self-government. Public sector jobs were sold frequently, to maintain the constantly depleted royal coffers. Corruption seemed to be the rule rather than the exception, even when high-profile officials were exposed to *visitas*, or unannounced visits from inspectors of the Crown, or to major audits, called *residencias*, at the end of their terms.

These ceremonies were often more a ritual formality than a meaningful investigation.

Justice was slow, tortuous, and imperfect. Legal proceedings took decades. Copious legislation, the difficulty of shipping voluminous documents and files back and forth, and the very nature of legal and administrative proceedings caused great delays. This may very well have given rise to the Spanish expression, "You will have lawsuits, even if you win them." Another saying wryly sums it up: "There are two types of legal problems: those that resolve themselves and those that have no solution." The Americans and the Spaniards on the other side of the Atlantic were convinced that there was no justice under the sun. This was a grave conclusion, for the most basic function of the king was to impart justice. Within the best Hispanic tradition, sovereignty was, strictly speaking, "jurisdiction," or the ability to apply the law and dictate just sentences throughout a territory. In Spain, sovereignty was functioning badly; in America, worse.

Where did the Laws of the Indies come from? Probably from the Roman tradition reflected in the Law of Castile and, more specifically, from the *Siete Partidas*, a code of laws compiled by Alfonso X, the Wise, in the thirteenth century to impose order on the chaos of medieval justice. Castilian Law was similar to but still significantly different from the law of Aragon, Navarre, or any other Iberian territory that was once independent or that had special codes. The Laws of the Indies, enacted specifically for the American territories, were meant to take into account, whenever possible, indigenous customs and institutions without relaxing control or ignoring the interests of the Crown. The final result, however, exposed a wide gap between the principles that inspired the laws of Spain — some dictated by moralists and theologians — and their actual application. The discrepancy gave rise to an uncomfortable, widespread feeling of defenselessness among the Americans. They sought justice from a distant king who either withheld it or took so long in granting it that it became worthless. Perhaps it was an impossible mission. In Seville, Valladolid, or Madrid — despite the great effort by Spanish officials to document all cases — America remained little more than an incomprehensible reality. Spain was equally an enigma to the Americans. In the 19th century, with a different meaning and in another context, Karl Marx coined a term that expresses this disengagement: alienation.

VICEROYALTIES, AUDIENCIAS, AND REPUBLICS

In the mid-16th century, Charles V, concerned by the challenges to his authority in America, decided to resurrect a bureaucratic hierarchy dating back to the Middle Ages — the viceroyalty (a role which Columbus had assumed in a more honorary than practical sense). This "substitute-king" was appointed for a limited time (lest he become too attached to his exalted position) and was endowed with almost all the attributes of the legitimate monarch and a good many of the symbols of his enormous power.

The viceroy would carry out his duties in the most opulent manner imaginable. Formalities were important, since they represented authority. Generally, the viceroy lived in an imposing palace surrounded by all kind of luxury and protected by regular soldiers, men paid for their service. During outdoor ceremonies, he appeared under a canopy and dressed ostentatiously. The army and clergy were arrayed as his subordinates. He was the *de facto* military, civil, and to a certain degree, religious leader, and his duties included appointing bishops and parish priests. He was greeted with respect and reverence. Like the king, the viceroy ruled a court of distinguished men. Mexico and Lima soon competed with Valladolid, Madrid, and Seville in pomp and refinement.

Some conquistadors were granted noble titles and coats of arms. For the Spanish, who were caught up in what French historian Bartolomé Bennasar has described as the "madness" of purity of blood and impeccable lineage, acquiring titles of nobility became an obsession. Many vied for years to obtain this recognition. The documents submitted to the king summarizing their merits were called *probanzas*, or writs of proof. The Crown, however, was not inclined to generosity, knowing that allowing the growth of a powerful, large, and wealthy nobility generally led to separatist plots. By the fifteenth century, every modern European monarchy had consolidated its power after weakening the aristocracy. Now, it would be foolish to feed a possible enemy in America. Still, some conquistadors got what they wanted. Hernán Cortés became governor and marquis of the Oaxaca Valley, and Charles V generously granted him 23,000 Indians, a fortune. He did not name Cortés viceroy, though; it would have been downright reckless to empower such an audacious, imaginative conspirator.

As centuries passed and decadence set in, the Crown became more "practical" and tolerant. It began selling aristocratic titles, but did not stop there. It also sold skin color, a practice introduced by Charles III. For a reasonable fee, an afflicted mestizo could "whiten" himself. Skin color was granted through decrees known as *cédulas de gracias al sacar*. It was not a matter of reducing pigmentation or changing features, but of buying eloquent parchments that declared blacks or mestizos white. Beginning in 1795, one could buy a dispensation from the "colored" state (called *pardo*) for 500 pesos. *Quinterones* (individuals who had one black ancestor in five generations) had to pay a little more, 800 pesos. Eventually, inflation caused by the wars with France forced a price hike: 700 pesos for *pardos*, 1,000 for *quinterones*. These transactions were not provoked solely (nor primarily) by social vanity. To attend a university, one had to be white. Having received such a decree, mulatto José de Azarza presented himself at the University of Bogotá in 1797, and the university was obliged to accept him. Academic authorities protested the indignity of his presence, but the Crown stood firm. The university finally admitted Azarza but made it clear that it would not repeat the concession.

Four viceroyalties were established and between 1535 and 1813, 170 appointees occupied them. Only four of these viceroys were born in Latin America, a fact that underlines the little confidence the Creoles inspired in the Spanish court. The first viceroyalty was formed in 1535 in New Spain (Mexico and Central America) and the second in Peru (Peru, Bolivia, Ecuador) in 1543. Much later, in 1717, came New Granada

(Colombia, Panama, Venezuela), followed in 1776 by La Plata (Argentina, Chile, Paraguay, Uruguay). By some alchemy, these four entities prefigured, or perhaps reflected, what later became four cultural regions, four repertoires of manners and gestures, and four ways of pronouncing Spanish, observed in today's Latin America. Certainly, a reasonably homogenized world exists across Mexico and Central America. Likewise, there is a Caribbean family along the coast of Colombia, Venezuela, Yucatan, the Greater Antilles — in Cuba, the Dominican Republic, and Puerto Rico — and Panama. The Andean region encompasses parts of Colombia, Venezuela, Ecuador, Peru, and Bolivia. To the south lie Argentina, Uruguay, Paraguay, and less conspicuously, Chile, with its amicable people and their curiously high-pitched inflections. These are not clear cultural or linguistic boundaries, but rather recognizable families sharing a common kinship. Novelist García Márquez, for example, considers himself more like a Cuban or Venezuelan than a *cachaco*, or a Bogotan. Though his native country is Colombia, his anthropological affiliation is Caribbean. He admits as much.

The 18 Latin American states of today, including Puerto Rico, originated from the *audiencia*, an institution created to govern and manage American territories. The primary role of the *audiencia* was to impart justice, but because the separation of powers was not a developed concept in the 16th and 17th centuries, it assumed the task of governing or advising those who governed. An *audiencia* could be one of three kinds: viceroyal, presided over by a viceroy; praetorian, commanded by a captain-general or governor; and subordinate, led by a distinguished official under the direct control of the viceroy. Many of the cities that accommodated *audiencias* later became the capitals of independent states: Mexico City, Guatemala City, Panama City, Lima, Bogotá, Caracas, Santo Domingo, Santiago, Quito, and Buenos Aires. The *audiencias* became a kind of training ground for independence. They conferred a status that could not be renounced easily. The officials who managed them became, sometimes without warning, a ruling class. Other countries formed from *gobernaciones*. These were territories like provinces run by *intendecias*, administrations created after Charles III implemented much-needed government reform in the second half of the 18th century. Ironically, the bureaucratic web woven to control and subjugate the Americans later became the lines of fracture and of flight that would lead to independence.

THE ENCOMIENDA AND ENCOMENDERO

Although it has been repeated ad nauseam, it is still astonishing that a mere 25,000 Spaniards managed to dominate 25 million natives during the first 70 years of the conquest, especially since many of the native groups, such as the Carib and Araucanian Indians, were fierce warriors. One way this control was achieved was through the medieval Spanish institution erected during the Reconquest known as the *commenda*, and later in the New World as the *encomienda*. The *encomienda* began with the arrival of Columbus and lasted until the mid-18th century. It provided for the compensation of nobles for present and future service through the personal taxes of the vanquished in conquered regions. This function — paying taxes to the *encomendero*, or the Spanish settler — would continue in America, with the addition of two others. The first was forced Indian labor for the benefit of the *encomendero* anywhere he chose: in the mine or on the hacienda as a worker or domestic servant. The second was the evangelization and transculturation of the natives by doctrinarian priests.

To force the natives to work, the Spaniards used ruthless overseers not averse to corporal punishment. Beatings were common. The monarchs and the Council of the Indies protested such mistreatment, but the monarchs were far away and had no impact on the rapidly spreading opinion that the whip was the best remedy for "Indian indolence." "Lazy" and "dimwits" were the standard descriptions for the conquered. Over time, mestizos increasingly filled the role of implacable foreman or boss. From the outset, a violent social stratification was formed where race determined one's position. It persists in large measure even today, at the dawn of the third millennium.

For an Indian, especially in rural areas (where the majority lived, despite feverish urbanization by the Spanish), the living representation of the state was the *encomendero*. While the laws referred to them as free vassals, in reality, the native Indians were kept in a kind of slavery. Harsh conditions were alleviated only if the *encomendero* chose to be generous. What is worse, even converting to Christianity, learning Spanish, and adopting a new culture did not guarantee the Indian's freedom. The *encomendero* could transfer him to his children, grandchildren, or great-grandchildren — the law authorized using Indians over four generations.

In addition to the *encomienda*, there were other means of exploiting the Indians. The *mita* was the Peruvian Indians' own system for allocating contract laborers (in which they drew lots to work in mines and on public works projects) and the Mexican Indians' *régimen de tandas* (work shifts). Of the two, the *mita* was the more complex. Its origins were Andean, born of the Incan need to complete or maintain their great public works, especially roads, bridges, granaries, and terraces for growing crops on mountainsides. The Incas used the *mita* to conscript their subjects into a kind of temporary public works service. The Spanish wasted no time in adopting this custom, introducing shorter work periods — the longest for 10 months of mine digging — and establishing a lottery to determine who would be a *mitayo* (Indian employed in the mines or public works). The Indians received a stipend for their work; though small, at least it was a form of wage. The Crown, as usual, dictated measures intended to relax the rigors suffered by the workers conscripted in the *mita*; perhaps the most interesting were those to protect women, especially pregnant women and mothers of small children. Some experts seek in these measures the birth of the modern labor rights movement; that is debatable, since medieval guilds also made similar provisions. Nevertheless, the measures reveal a sincere ethical interest in the fate of the unfortunate Indians.

41

3. Blacks in a Persistently Racist Society

We already know that Indians, mestizos, and even white Creoles never accepted the state the Spanish Crown imposed in America without great reservations. We also know that it felt less like a common home and more like a painful corset inflicting alien discomfort and restriction. But what happened to the blacks? Their memory of African institutions finally erased, was not America the only homeland possible?

Witnessing the happy excesses of Brazil's carnivals, blazing with beautiful women of all possible ethnic mixes (a large percentage of them black or mulatto), you might think the country is an amiable racial melting pot. Moreover, if you talk to people, you might well get the impression that the most beloved Brazilian hero is the soccer star Pelé. Not that this is a uniquely Brazilian phenomenon — Cubans also universally admire "Duke" Hernandez, Cuban pitcher for the New York Yankees. Both are magnificent athletes and both are black, which might suggest that Latin America enjoys greater racial harmony than the United States. Actually, a different type of racism prevails.

Practiced through segregationist laws, racism was blatant and institutionalized in the United States until the 1960s, recalling a kind of South African apartheid. By the end of the decade, the civil rights struggle had brought about the integration of public institutions and affirmative action measures intended to achieve "racial balance," or the representation of blacks and other minorities proportionate to their demographic weight. South of the Rio Grande, anti-black racism is no longer institutionalized, either. Nevertheless, racism persists in society. Latin Americans prefer to ignore it and pretend that it does not exist, but it is there. It is present where scarcely any blacks are seen — in Argentina, Mexico, and Bolivia, for example — and in more pronounced and diverse forms where blacks make up a substantial part of the population — in places such as Cuba, the Dominican Republic, Panama, the coast of Colombia, and Puerto Limón in Costa Rica.

It is not just discrimination perpetrated by racist whites. At the close of the last century, noted Dominican politician and Social Democrat Jose Peña Gomez never reached power because, among other reasons, he was too dark in a primarily mulatto society. His blackness threatened many of his fellow Dominicans. Until mid-century, in Cuba, blacks were denied entrance to luxury hotels and casinos. Nat King Cole experienced this discrimination first hand, as did Louis Armstrong in Caracas. Blacks and mulattos had their separate social and cultural gatherings. A common expression from those times stated that each race should *know its place*, and the question of one's race came down to a matter of shades of brown. After the 1959 establishment of an egalitarian communist society in Cuba, racist practices should have ended, but they did not. Forty years after Castro gained control, in a country where half the population is black or mulatto, almost the entire power structure and military hierarchy is still white, while blacks remain visibly poorer than other Cubans.

SLAVES IN SPAIN

Where in Spain did each race, each shade of skin belong? How did these groups form? Naturally, this social phenomenon takes us back to slavery, the origin of which had more to do with the outcome of war than with race. Slavery was prevalent in Spain, as in almost all of Europe, from ancient times well into the 19th century, although it decreased drastically during the eighteenth. In some ways, according to anthropologists, the appearance of slavery was a step forward. Prior to slavery, prisoners of war were killed and even eaten. Once they were found to be more useful as a work force than a source of protein, they were made into servants and allowed to live. In its Latin origin the word's meaning expresses this concept: "servant" comes from *servus*, the common root of *servere*, to save. (At least, so explains University of Minnesota history professor William D. Phillips, Jr., author of an excellent overview of the history of slavery in Spain.)

Under Roman rule, slavery in Spain multiplied exponentially. Survivors from Iberian towns who resisted the advancing legions were sold as slaves and remained permanently in this condition, except for those able to buy their own manumission with the savings of the *peculium*, personal money accumulated from extra work done outside the master's estate. Apparently, very few managed to buy their freedom, and most ended up at the large state-run mines. Roman slaves could, indeed, be owned by individuals or the state. They were treated like objects or animals. An agricultural expert of Hispanic origin, Columela, referred to them as *talking tools*. These "tools" could be exploited without limit. Even Emperor Constantine, despite his famous edict on tolerance in religious matters — which eventually resulted in the conversion of the Roman Empire to Christianity — authorized the brutal punishment of slaves, as his predecessors had done. If any died as a result, no responsibility existed for the master. He had simply lost something that belonged to him.

It was thought for some time that the influence of the Stoics, who believed in the fraternity of all men, and the subsequent arrival of Christianity, had been deterrents to slavery, but documented proof points in another direction. The Catholic Church did not oppose slavery; it only requested more humane treatment for its victims, as it made clear at the first Council of Toledo (397-400). The Church needed slaves to work monastic lands. Slaves could not be ordained as priests or nuns because as another's property, they lacked the proper moral autonomy to make the decision to serve God. (Aristotle's theory of slaves by natural law had not yet been debunked.) Still, while Christians could own slaves who had embraced the faith, Jews were forbidden to own slaves baptized in the Christian faith.

With the establishment of the Visigoth kingdom in Spain in the fifth century, no great changes took place in the conscription or treatment of war prisoners as slaves. The penal code, however, added three new categories of free individuals who could be enslaved: rapists of free women, kidnappers of children, and adulteresses. In addition, within his diocese a bishop could condemn to slavery a priest's lover, and kings had the same right with those who denied them aid in times of war. Desperately poor people could also sell themselves into slavery to survive, while others could become slaves if they were unable to satisfy debts to individuals or the state.

Although the treatment of slaves continued to be merciless, the Visigoths introduced some compassionate measures. Before mutilating a slave — cutting off a hand, foot, tongue, ear, or testicle — one had to get authorization from a highly placed person, such as a duke or count. It was forbidden to kill innocent slaves, although proof of their guilt could be brought forth after the sentence was fulfilled. Whoever killed another's slave had to compensate the wronged party with a clearly specified fine, for among the Visigoths, every person had a price, or *wergeld*. Value varied according to certain factors, including sex and age. Free men were worth much more than slaves. An old female slave was worth very little; it was cheaper to eliminate her and pay the *wergeld* than to maintain her.

At the end of the seventh century, the Church became more generous and permitted some slaves to be ordained as deacons or priests. They were not granted freedom, however, nor were they allowed as easily to become monks. In any case, churches became a refuge to slaves fleeing particularly ferocious owners. A law established by the Council of Lerida (546) forbade clergy from whipping slaves — who would have sought sanctuary in other churches and monasteries. At that time, for a church to be considered a parish it needed a minimum of 10 slaves, an obvious incentive to add to its group of captives.

The Muslim conquest of nearly all of Spain in the eighth century had important consequences from an ethnic point of view. Among the Berber and Arab troops that crossed the Mediterranean were black soldiers, probably slaves. In the Islamic world, the use of captives in special military units or as officials, even of high social standing, was a frequent practice derived from a logical observation: when unattached to local groups, strangers tend to be loyal to a power that employs and repays them. Thus originated, for example, the terrifying Turkish *Mamluks* who had such an important impact on the eastern Mediterranean. But if the black soldiers appointed to the Islamic army were conspicuous, just as outstanding was the number of Christians quickly forced into slavery by the invaders. Some 150,000 were made slaves, 30,000 (or 20 percent) of which were sent to the caliph of Baghdad as a kind of *quinto real*. The Muslims had adopted the same mathematical rule to dispense their war booty. They normally distributed the slaves according to the extent of resistance they had shown invaders. Those who submitted were generally well treated. The *Mozarabs* (Christians living in Islamic Spanish territories) could maintain their properties, including their slaves, when and if the latter did not follow Islam. They paid, of course, a per capita tax to the new rulers. Slaves cost them half the worth of a free person.

Unlike what was happening in the Spanish-Roman or Spanish-Visigoth world (two ways of referring to Christian Spain), in Al-Andalus (as the Islamic area was named), slaves were directed to domestic service, or under the right conditions, to administrative work. Women, if attractive, became prostitutes or were placed in a harem — the feminine enclosure within a home, similar to the Greek gynaeceum — watched over by slave eunuchs and reserved for the enjoyment of the more important males. When they aged, or if they were unattractive, they were used as nannies. Curiously, from a modern perspective, slave women had more freedoms than the supposedly free women of the Islamic world, since a strict view of female chastity turned Muslim women into prisoners in their own draped homes and in clothing that hid them almost entirely from the public eye. By contrast, slave women, like the courtesans of the Greeks, learned to play musical instruments, and as

47

mere objects of male pleasure often enjoyed fewer restrictions than free women. None of this is to say, of course, that the treatment given slaves was better in Al-Andalus than in the Christian kingdoms forming to the north. Though the Koran forbade mistreating and assaulting captives, there were frequent flagellations, mutilations (usually of nose or ears), and fatal incidents of dragging prisoners tethered to horses.

As the Spanish-Muslim world consolidated, the number of black slaves it imported increased. Shipped from Islamic North Africa by skillful Arab slave traders who either captured them in violent *razzias*, or raids, or bought them from black intermediaries, they were often exchanged for salt, weapons, and fabrics. How many blacks have been enslaved or bought by North African Arabs since the seventh century? Historian Ralph A. Austen cites a chilling figure: close to seven-and-a-half million. How many died in the caravans crossing the Sahara, exposed to a killer sun with little or no water and freezing nights? There is no knowing; but there are reasons to believe that this terrifying journey was no more merciful than the Atlantic crossings that later lost as much as 30 percent of their human cargo. Such data is apparently disowned or ignored by those African-Americans who, since the 1960s, have hoped to find in Islam and Arab culture a historical memory more compassionate and hospitable to their own ethnicity.

The Spanish military effort to regain Moorish-ruled territory resulted in the perpetuation of slavery, fueled by the prisoners of war each camp gained. As the Christians extended the perimeter of their conquests, Muslim slaves became the majority. Unlike the practices of the Roman or Visigoth eras, the Christian kingdoms did not employ slaves in exhausting mine work, but rather used them as servants and household assistants, as farm laborers (who gradually developed a serfdom similar to feudalism), and as artisans of carpentry, construction, blacksmithing, and weaving.

Five events at the end of the fifteenth century proved fatal for black Africans. First, the Portuguese colonized a large portion of Africa's Atlantic coast. The improvement of navigational techniques made possible the gradual exploration of Africa and the establishment of permanent commercial stations and slave houses, gradually converted into centers for the purchase, classification, and exportation of captured "pieces." The Portuguese raids were backed by bulls that Pope Nicholas V (1454) and Pope Calixtus III (1456) issued legitimizing the enslavement of blacks if it also included converting the "possessed idolaters." Second, Slavs from eastern Europe were progressively converted to Christianity, making their enslavement difficult for theological reasons. Third, the Ottoman Turks' conquest of Constantinople in 1453 created in the east Mediterranean a Muslim power so strong that slave raids became impossible. Fourth, the harvest of the sugar cane crop required a superior physical strength much easier to draw from a slave than a free farm worker. Fifth, the final routing of the Muslims from the kingdom of Granada in 1492 dried up one of the main sources of slave labor since the treaties of surrender included an agreement to respect Arabs' freedom. Though Christians later broke almost all of the pact's conditions, at the first moment of the conquest and colonization of America — performed by a Spanish society convinced of the essential indignity of manual labor — it seemed inevitable that the "dark continent" would be turned tragically into the supplier of human flesh for the cruelest, longest mass exploitation recorded in history.

SLAVES IN AMERICA

In 1517 Fray Bartolomé de Las Casas, appalled by the treatment of the natives in the New World, proposed that every white man residing in the Indies import 12 black slaves to relieve the locals of the crushing work imposed by the Spanish. On ethical-religious grounds, Las Casas had no objection to slavery. Leviticus, in the Bible, permitted slavery. But a peculiar personal circumstance may have also been a factor. A Sevillian like Las Casas was probably accustomed to seeing black slaves and viewed it as natural. Black slaves were a familiar part of Andalusian life inherited from the Arabs. In his native town alone, there were some 15,000. At least one of them, Juan de Valladolid, had been accorded a

49

certain nobility and was named judge to oversee disputes among blacks. Several decades later, another black slave known as Juan Latino became one of the most respected scholars in Spain and earned a professorship at the University of Granada. He was called an "Ethiopian," but the slave *castas*, or nations, were very difficult to pinpoint because of communication problems. *Ethiopian* was probably a generic categorization to describe blacks.

Of those castas, the black slaves came from what today are called Senegal, Biafra, Ghana, Nigeria, Benin, Togo Dahomey, Cameroon, Congo, Gabon, Angola, and Mozambique, although the bulk of them were most likely taken from the vast zone known as the Gulf of Guinea. All were referred to as *bozales*, or simpletons. Even as early as the 16th century, the commercial value of this traffic superseded that of gold or spices, a fact that worried the Spanish since, according to the 1494 Treaty of Tordesillas, slave trade was an exclusive privilege ceded by the Pope to the Portuguese. Still, some thinkers (among the most notable of whom were Tomás Mercado and Luis de Molina) condemned the practice on moral and philosophical grounds. We will return to these two important thinkers in Chapter 5, "An Economy Twisted at Birth."

In essence, black slavery became a theological debate just as the enslavement of the native Americans had done, with defenders such as Portuguese Duarte Pacheco Pereira and opponents such as Bartolomé Frías de Albornoz, professor of law at the University of Mexico who dared refute the Church's reading of Aristotle. No justification could be found within a Christian ethic for enslaving primitive peoples who had never heard the word of God, Albornoz argued. The Inquisition placed his book of 1573, *The Art of Contracts*, on the *Index* of forbidden texts and kept it there for many years.

If the Spanish could not take part in the capture and transportation of slaves, known as "traffic" or "trade," because that business had been granted to Portugal through the Papal Bulls, nothing prevented them from buying or reselling slaves. It was a bustling business whose exclusivity — through the *asiento* (contract) or *derecho real* (royal right) to acquire a certain number of slaves — frequently became a fruitful source of privileges. Asked how he made his fortune, the famous Spanish-Cuban slaver Julián Zulueta replied, "Buying whites in Spain and selling blacks in America." Nevertheless, even the Portuguese monopoly on the traffic disappeared at a key moment in 1578 when King Sebastian died without heirs, allowing Philip II to annex Portugal. The Portuguese continued to be traffickers, but Portugal was now a part of Spain and every aspect of the business was handled in the combined territories.

The situation changed again when Portugal broke off from Spain in 1640. Philip IV, now monarch in Madrid, decided to punish the Portuguese by canceling the privilege of supplying African slaves to Spanish possessions in America. He did not, however, give up Spain's practice of acquiring new slaves. Where and how would he get them, now? Dealing with the English, Dutch, and French was a viable alternative, but with the first two raised a moral problem: the English were Protestants, and some Dutch traders were Jews with property in Curaçao. Their slaves were dangerously tainted with Protestantism and Judaism. The Crown was disconcerted by the prospect of trading with the mortal enemies of Catholic Spain. Still, the only option was trade, whether through legal or illegal channels. What was important was to avoid either slowing the flow of slaves who advanced the production of sugar and mined the metals, or losing the tax money gained with every transaction of human flesh. The Inquisition would have to take upon itself the task of defending against threats to Catholicism, keeping theological doctrine intact.

Black slaves were treated considerably worse than even the Indians. The original sources were primarily African tribes who would capture their enemies, although sometimes, European blacks participated in the *razzias*. British historian Hugh Thomas has related an account of King Tegbesu of Dahomey in the mid-18th century receiving 250,000 pounds sterling from traders for the permanent supply of captives to Europeans. Was Tegbesu a traitor to the men and women of his race? For him, blackness was not a consideration. Capturing an enemy and selling or trading him was an old tradition. Sometimes the same captors were themselves seized and sold. Being black created no special bond. It was precisely the same case as the Genoese or Catalonian traders who sold captive Greeks and Slavs. For them, being white created no moral obligation. For black Africans as well as whites, there were friendly and hostile nations, and it was perfectly legitimate to enslave the enemy.

After their capture on African soil, enslaved blacks had to walk, sometimes for weeks, to the ports of embarkation. Shackled and extremely malnourished, they were loaded onto slave ships designed to store hundreds of "pieces" in their holds. They lay pressed against each other with barely room to squirm amid vomit, urine, and feces, frightened out of their wits and whipped into submission. Thirty percent or sometimes more died on a voyage. Others went blind from infections and still others were simply thrown overboard without a second thought.

When the cargo reached America, it was usually inspected by a physician or medical authority of some sort who generally decreed a quarantine if too many were sick or seemed to be in worse health than usual. Afterwards, the *asentista*, or contractor — who had legal sanction to import slaves — paid the custom house entitlement fees and then "sealed" the transaction with a branding iron, burning the initials of the importing owner into the slaves' skin, usually on the back or shoulders. This mark not only showed who the owner was, but it also certified that the transaction was legal. Afterwards, in chains, the slaves were locked in dark, unsanitary barracks until the day of the sale. Once sold, they resumed the journey to their fated destination. The new master would re-brand them to establish his ownership in a decisive manner.

For the most part, slaves were submitted to heartless treatment in the houses and on the plantations where they were sent, where they were severely punished for any infraction. They were barely allowed to have any sexual contact. The males and females lived separately, and there were fewer black women than men, nor were males permitted intercourse with Indian women, although some risked it. The punishment could be as much as 100 lashes or, as happened in Chile, castration. And, heaven forbid a black man be heard complimenting a white woman. In one documented case, a slave in Montevideo was given 200 lashes for making flattering remarks to a Creole woman.

Sometimes the tortures exceeded human tolerance. In his book, *The African Experience in Spanish America*, Leslie B. Rout recounts the story of Pedro Gilafo, an unfortunate black whose owner had him boiled alive in front of the other slaves. Gilafo had tried to escape and his master found it convenient to make an example of him.

Even so, slaves occasionally did rebel and escape. They formed fugitive camps, with palisades, which the slave holders would attack with their packs of hunting dogs. Several fugitives were so adept at evading their owners that they became popular legends, among them Juan Andresote of Venezuela, Diego Bioho of Cartagena, and Ñianga in Mexico. Some slave camps in remote areas, such as a camp in the Dutch colony of Surinam, were never vanquished.

Despite all the authorities' efforts to keep blacks from engaging in interracial sexual relations, mixing did occur. The racist eye of the period took great care to distinguish between the various gradations and combinations: black and white — *mulatto;* white and mulatto — *cuarterón,* white and cuarterón — *quinterón;* white and *quinterón* — white again. There were also the black variations: black and mulatto — *zambo;* black and zambo — *zambo prieto;* black and *zambo prieto* — black again. Then there were the black-Indian mixtures: black and Indian — *mulatto pardo;* mulatto pardo and Indian — *lobo;* lobo and mulatto pardo — *coyote.* Naturally, this classification differed from country to country. In Mexico, a union between a *morisco,* or a Christianized moor, and a Spanish woman produced a *chino.* When the Indian mated with a chino, they made a *salto atrás* ("step back"). There were two unions even more curiously named: *tente en el aire* ("stay up in the air") and *no te entiendo* ("I don't understand you").

The Church became a spiritual and physical refuge for blacks, as it had been for the Indians; but it stopped short of renouncing its ownership of slaves. The most extreme example was in Chile, where until their expulsion at the end of the 18th century the Jesuits were the greatest slaveholders. Every church or monastery counted on its quota of slaves, who were generally better treated than those owned by laymen and encouraged to organize black fraternities for religious processions and festivals.

Some slave owners were too squeamish to punish disobedient or unruly slaves as severely as custom recommended. To ease their conscience, in some places, such as Havana, they could go to whipping sites where, for a modest sum, one could take the insubordinate slave to be flogged by a man whose job it was. For its part, the Holy Inquisition, ever vigilant in guarding religious doctrine, added its weight by persecuting those who openly practiced their pagan rituals.

The Church oversaw medical care and burials, and it also ran the educational system. Bit by bit, and almost always within strict racial segregation, blacks received a very rudimentary education as part of their elemental Christian development. In Córdoba, Argentina, in 1782, the pious bishop Jose Antonio de Alberto decreed that girls' orphanages could receive a four percent quota of "blacks, zambas, and other inferior classes" and authorized boys' orphanages to accept ten percent. Although small, it was a step forward. As they grew, the black and mulatto orphans, both boys and girls, became the servants of the white orphans, at their sexual disposal. Colored orphans received only very elementary instruction; it was not acceptable for blacks to acquire a cultural education. At least one mulatto was punished with a whipping for having learned to read and write without his owner's permission.

The Spanish and Creole preoccupation with establishing rigid, unbending hierarchies and monopolies based on origin was particularly harmful to blacks. There were many jokes about their supposed stupidity. Unless a white man accompanied them, black women could not wear silk dresses or jewelry. Even then, there were exceptions, as Eugenia Montilla found out in Córdoba in 1750 after accepting a white family's invitation to a reception. For daring to dress like a white woman, she was stripped naked and flogged, and her clothes were burned.

There was no underestimating white ire or vigilance of segregationist rules and norms. When mulatto Juan Morelos finally achieved the title of tax collector in 1785, he was accused of inappropriately affixing the word *don* before his name. Small wonder that a century earlier, in 1688, a royal decree had prohibited blacks from studying at the university. To enter, it was necessary to show proof of "clean blood," which blacks and mulattos obviously could not do, just as they could not, even if they had been freed, live in the same neighborhood as whites. Blacks lived in extraordinarily poor neighborhoods, ghettos where they had to stay indoors after dark upon the sounding of a trumpet or bells. That is how it was in the beautiful Colombian city, Cartagena of the Indies.

In 1789, while the French Revolution raged, the Spanish Crown drafted the *Codigo negro carolino*, a set of laws intended to humanize the treatment of slaves. It demanded total submission to slave owners, but it also created a judicial body, the *procurador de negros*, to defend the rights of slaves. This may appear to have been a small concession, but it signaled the explicit recognition that slaves were not objects but human beings.

Whether Spanish-Portuguese slavery in Latin America was worse than the English, French, and Dutch slavery is an old issue, the crux of a debate that has evoked sound arguments to sustain all opinions. It seems the procedures used by all Europeans were very similar. They all captured slaves in Africa, hunted them down as if they were animals, branded them, punished them brutally, and segregated them from other races and from the opposite gender. The inhuman Atlantic crossings in slave ships occurred under every flag. The use of black women as sex objects by white men, sometimes for their own pleasure, other times for prostitution, was perpetrated more frequently by the whites of Catholic countries — Spain, Portugal, and France — but it also took place in the Protestant territories. After all, even Martin Luther, whose mindset was inevitably shaped by the times he lived in, thought that without the slave work force the economic fabric of Europe could collapse.

The type of work they were given largely determined the hardships the slave suffered. If he was doomed to cut sugar cane — a desperately exhausting job carried out in tropical heat, under a broiling sun and under the constant attack of mosquitoes — his predicament was frightful. For the Cuban sugarcane farmers — callous masters who sought profit above all else — a slave's useful lifespan consisted of about five or six years of intense labor. Owners, therefore, whipped slaves into working between 18 and 20 hours a day. A similar fate awaited the mine laborers. For those slaves who worked harvesting coffee or cacao beans or picking cotton or tobacco leaves, the rhythm and style of labor permitted less barbarous treatment.

There is, however, one incontrovertible point of distinction: in 1807, England became the first great European power to renounce the slave trade (Denmark had done so in 1792). It employed its own Royal Navy to impose the import prohibition on other nations and to back the agreements of the 1815 Congress of Vienna. (The new laws did nothing to stop the breeding and sale of slaves already in the Americas.) In the meantime, Spain and Portugal — despite Spain's having received 400,000 pounds sterling from the British treasury for eliminating the slave trade and compensating slave owners — did everything possible to continue the infamous commerce, encouraged by the Creoles of Cuba and Brazil. Not until 1886 did Madrid abolish slavery, and Brazil held out for two more years. The last ship carrying slaves arrived in Cuba in 1870, five years after the abolition of slavery in the United States and decades after Spain had promised to halt the traffic. Even after that date, some slave smugglers mocked international vigilance and reached Brazil.

Did England act out of economic interest, or was the main motivation moral? Most cynical scholars say the Industrial Revolution simply made the system obsolete, and it was an irresistible opportunity to make the recently lost colonies in North America look bad. Nonetheless, the moral question appears to have had great influence on England's political change. In 1783, British Quakers launched a campaign that led to the creation of the Abolition Society. Over the next few decades, the abolitionists' clamor grew, until they managed to reach the hearts of some important politicians, such as Lord Palmerston, prime minister of the British Empire (1855-65). Nor was this the first time that a change of sensibility took place in the West. The drive toward tolerance and respect for human rights began in Europe at the end of the 16th century. In the period of the Enlightenment, Montesquieu — even while theorizing over state structures in *The Spirit of Laws* — found time to condemn slavery.

How many Africans were subjugated and sent across the Atlantic to endure the horrors of slavery? Hugh Thomas cites something over 11 million. Four million went to Brazil, two and a half million to the Spanish possessions (especially Cuba), two million to the English Caribbean, over a million and a half to French colonies, a half million to the Dutch, another half million to the United States and British Canada, and some 200,000 to the European islands in the Atlantic (the Canaries, the Azores, and others). This human mass of staggering proportion was consigned to work as follows: five million to sugar cane fields, two million to coffee plantations, one million to the mines, two million to domestic service, a half million to cotton, a quarter million to cacao fields, and a quarter million to construction.

REPUBLICS AND SLAVES

At the end of the 18th century, vague, disquieting news reached the slaves, as well as the Creoles and Spanish. Each group reacted differently — the Creoles and whites with trepidation and the slaves with concealed excitement. In 1791, on the heels of the French Revolution, slaves under the leadership of Toussaint Louverture had revolted in the Caribbean colony of Haiti. At the time, Haiti was one of the richest agricultural areas in the world (with a value of production higher than Canada's). Slavery was its backbone. A half million Africans and their descendants were exploited by 25,000 French colonists.

In 1803, Napoleon's army, racked by tropical diseases and losing strength due to the resistance of these insurgents in Haiti, was called back to Europe. The emperor had more pressing concerns. The men sailed for Europe, leaving the rebels with a victory. Toussaint died just months before, in a French prison cell, without witnessing his triumph. On January 1, 1804, the first black republic in history was erected in Haiti. Thousands of embarrassed and chagrined whites and mulattos fled the island, fearing reprisals, and word of this debacle quickly spread throughout the world.

For the blacks of Latin America, it was a miracle beyond belief. The Creoles had mixed feelings. They welcomed the news that a great European army had been defeated by irregular troops, but the thought that slaves were capable of rising up in arms and pursuing their own independent goals terrified them. And the Haitian slaves had not distinguished between Creole and French when they struck with their razor-sharp machetes — they attacked all the whites, who, to their minds, were all slave owners. For the Spanish, this was a particularly bloodcurdling prospect. Napoleon's armies had been invincible in Europe up to then; how had they been beaten by a few thousand slaves with little military experience and no education? What would keep the same thing from happening in the Spanish colonies?

The tensions among all ethnicities were enormous. Just 150,000 Spaniards, who were generally unhappy with the Crown's management of its American territories, controlled several million Latin Americans. The American-born whites felt oppressed, usurped by the Spaniards who occupied almost all of the important public posts. At the base of the pyramid, powerless and humiliated and bearing the weight of all those above them, were the mestizos and Indians, and still further down, the black slaves. The elements were in place for a major conflagration. The spark would soon come.

The first signs of an impending racial conflict were seen in Buenos Aires. The English took the city in 1806, prompting a black rebellion. A prominent Creole, Juan Martín de Pueyrredón, faced the invaders and asked them to force the slaves to submit anew to their owners. Not wishing to alienate the good will of the local businessmen, the British complied. Soon afterward, the English were defeated by troops under Creole Santiago Liniers (who was named military chief after the disgraceful flight of the viceroy). However, they returned the following year with an army of 12,000 men. Now, the desperate Creoles recruited slave and free blacks — with 100 lashes or threats of perpetual slavery for those failing to appear at the barracks. The blacks fought valiantly, despite the opinion of Argentine aristocrat Manuel Belgrano that they were "cowardly and bloodthirsty."

The experience taught José de San Martín to incorporate blacks and coloreds into his army. They were especially useful in the battle of Maipú, which sealed the independence of Chile. Later, Sucre in Bolivia and Juan José Flores in Ecuador followed suit, though the Creole society was not very warm to the idea of arming large numbers of blacks and mulattos. Uruguayan Gervasio Artigas marched into exile in Paraguay with a predominantly mulatto and black guard. Although Bolívar, San Martin, Miranda were anti-slavery, independence was their main priority. Therefore, they avoided confrontation with the Creole slave owners. The Spanish took note of these contradictions and used them to their advantage. A good portion of the troops under Tomás Boves, the Spanish officer who first (and very successfully) suppressed the rebellion of Bolívar and Miranda were black and mulatto rangers. Bolívar himself, who in 1816 decreed the abolition of slavery in Great Colombia, could not avoid certain racial conflicts in his own ranks. Fearing a government of mulattos, he ordered the execution of some of his own men, among them mulatto general Manuel de Piar and black admiral José Padilla.

The republics, then, did not become a homeland for Latin American blacks until they had undergone a long, painful process of ups, downs, and frequent reversals. In Ecuador, the conclusive law abolishing slavery was only proclaimed in 1847, Colombia in 1851, Argentina in 1853, and Peru in 1855. In the still Spanish-ruled Cuba, it was not decreed until 1886. When it passed, Creole landowners arranged to import Chinese laborers into a work regime similar to the slaves.' Blacks were finally accepted as citizens, albeit of a second-class variety. A republican society that had inherited colonial values held them in great contempt.

This republican racism manifested itself in a migratory political movement intended to *whiten* the different nations by importing European youth. When Alberdi, an Argentine, declared, "To govern is to populate," he meant to populate with white Europeans — and he thought it better that they come from Italy rather than Spain. Fellow Argentine Domingo Faustino Sarmiento, for whom Alberdi held little regard, said something very similar in the last book he wrote, *Conflicts and Harmonies of the Races in America.*

It was a time when racism had attained a scientific sheen. The closing 18th century opened the way for polygenesis, which took as its premise the idea that human beings did not descend from a common ancestor — as the Bible proposed and genetics suggested — but from several sources, thus explaining the different practical results of the distinct races. It was a matter of biological determinism: some races were destined to win because they were endowed with greater capacity, while others were condemned to backwardness. In a way, the rise of polygenesis was a return to Aristotle and the changeless *nature* of human groups. The theory's most ardent champion in the Western Hemisphere was the prolific French writer (and diplomat in Brazil, where he may have reached his worst conclusions) Joseph-Arthur Gobineau, author of the nefarious and influential "Essay on the Inequality of Human Races," published in Paris in the early 1850s. One of Gobineau's most avid readers was Hitler, who remained convinced of the inherent superiority of the Aryan race.

The first half of the 20th century was hardly more generous to Latin American blacks. A racial war in Cuba in 1912 known as the "Little War of Blacks" was provoked by several ex-combatants of the Independence War (1895-1898) who wanted to create a colored political party. The independence struggle had left more than 3,000 black and mulatto dead, two-thirds of them assassinated by the army outside of combat. In Venezuela, Laureano Vallenilla Lanz, a brilliant intellectual in the service of dictator Juan Vicente Gómez (1908-1935), in his *Democratic Caesarism* defended the same racist ideas as Sarmiento, only more bluntly. He suggested that countries with the racial composition of Latin America had no future. The only thing that could save them was an alliance between a national intelligentsia of European descent and a dictator, or Caesar, capable of imposing order by the sword. A decade later, in the 1940s, this belief was implicitly sustained by Panamanian President Arnulfo Arias when, backed by popular support, he proposed denying citizenship to immigrant blacks who arrived to work in the construction of the Panama Canal.

This was not the only racist society in the area. Until then, Costa Rican blacks, nearly all of whom lived in or near Puerto Limón, were required to get a special permit before they could relocate to San José, the white and democratic capital. In Santo Domingo, in the 1930s, racism probably reached its highest point when young dictator Rafael Leonidas Trujillo ordered the army to assassinate several thousand Haitian peasants, most of them illegal immigrants in the Dominican Republic. The majority of Dominicans excused the act as a reprisal for the atrocities committed by Haitian troops during their occupation of Santo Domingo in the previous century.

At the outset of the 21st century, the integration of blacks and mulattos into Latin American society has made significant headway. No one now denies blacks the right to education. Almost everyone recognizes their contributions to the world of popular music and sports — a fact that perhaps increases the risk of creating another form of prejudice — and their great spiritual influence in religious matters, particularly in countries such as Brazil, Cuba, and the Dominican Republic, where faiths of African origin have attained a growing presence. There is still, however, a very clear relationship between one's skin color and one's socio-economic position, despite striking exceptions.

Why has the process of bringing equality between blacks and whites proven so difficult? An investigation in the 1960s by a United States sociologist and ex-Harvard professor, the former New York senator Daniel Patrick Moynihan, may apply to Latin America, as well as in his own country. Centuries of slavery gave way to single-parent households run by women of very limited economic means. Besides the undeniable white prejudice, unstructured households lacking the presence of responsible fathers deprived children of the necessary role models to inspire them and to impose constructive authority that would guide them to studies and a solid work ethic.

However, it is essential to point out that, in general, descendants of slaves brought up in the British cultural tradition exhibit better economic performance than descendants in the Spanish world or the US. Such is the case in Trinidad, the Bahamas, Barbados, and even the poorest country, Jamaica, along with the rest of the small English islands of the Lesser Antilles. Is it the result of British-made institutions and better education, or of societies where blacks are the dominant majority and therefore have a more positive self-image, where they are unimpeded by limitations or invisible psychological barriers to their social advancement? Several American sociologists and economists have noted the success of black Anglo-Caribbean immigrants in places where the African American population tends to be particularly poor, such as Miami. Black immigrants from Barbados have been among the most economically successful to arrive in the United States in the last hundred years. This fact undermines any theory that some races could be genetically predisposed to success or failure. Individual attitudes, customs, and values — what could collectively be referred to as culture — intertwined with history seem to determine economic success or failure for societies and people.

In any case, whether the reason cited by Moynihan is the principal cause or just one cause of the relative poverty of the black or mulatto population in Latin America, it is certain that this debate has not been granted the importance and priority it should command. Some may believe that discussing or exploring this divisive phenomenon could somehow contribute to promoting it, but the exact opposite is true. The only way to master an angry bull is to take it decisively by the horns. The issue of race is especially important because like a heavy burden, it weighs down on the institutional instability and divisiveness that already impairs the region.

4. Sex, Sexism, and Gender Roles

In Nicaragua, the transition from the Sandinista dictatorship to a democracy (1990-96) was conducted adroitly by a woman of delicate frame and iron will, Violeta Chamorro. At the end of the 1990s, Panamanians elected Mireya Moscoso president. Thirty years earlier, Argentines had done the same with Isabelita Perón (although the outcome was tragic). In Bolivia, Moira Paz Estenssoro, daughter of the legendary politician, promoted herself as the leader best fit to revitalize the party founded by her father. In the Dominican Republic, an outstanding woman, Milagros Ortiz Bosch, was elected vice president in 2000 — unsurprisingly so, perhaps, since during the government of Miguel Ángel Rodríguez in Costa Rica, two impressive, competent women had occupied the vice presidencies as well. In Ecuador, business mogul Joyce Ginatta from Guayaquil coordinated a campaign that forced the government to convert to a dollar economy. Many more examples could be listed. There is ample proof that in Latin America, women's progress in public life is increasing by leaps and bounds, just as it is in the European Union, the United States, and Canada. Even so, the situation for the majority of women has not changed substantially. The truth is that for most women, particularly the poorer and less educated ones, the situation is as bad today as it was centuries ago.

How did sexual (and sexist) roles and attitudes in Latin America develop? One of Latin Americans' most unfortunate contributions to the world is the word *macho* and its corresponding stereotype. It is easy to think the concept is of Spanish origin, especially since Spain gave birth to the figure of Don Juan (first through the pen of dramatist Tirso de Molina, then through dramatist and poet Zorrilla). But the actual "macho" image has little to do with that gallant libertine of the Golden Age. In our day it is more commonly associated with a mustachioed Mexican or an Argentine "Latin lover," complete with hairy chest, well-tended hair, and the reputation of being indefatigable in bed. Or, alternately, the word is linked to the romantic image of a bearded guerrilla warrior in perpetual combat against the military, another type of "macho" that caricaturists tend to portray in rather sinister fashion. These and many more represent typical variations of the Latin American stereotype.

The macho — to judge by hit songs, popular cinema, and television soap operas — is a womanizer who loves to drink and argue and will fight to defend his territory. He hates homosexuals and makes fun of them — rude jokes are popular in Ibero-American culture — partly in order to highlight his own masculinity. When he fathers children, he demands their obedience through intimidation and physical punishment. His woman is not really a companion or lover, but a possession, a dehumanized object to be ordered about and who must respond with veneration as well as total obedience. She attends to him through constant domestic work and sexual service on demand that must, of course, be absolutely exclusive. She is assumed to be gossipy, frivolous, and insipid and should be ignored, for she rarely has anything interesting to say. The macho, after all, finds it distasteful that his woman be more intelligent or better educated. All too frequently, when they argue, it is common for the man to make a final point with an act of physical or verbal violence against the woman. The "machos" of the world, not just the Latin American archetype, beat or insult their women without remorse.

What I have described so far is a caricature, a mixture of scoundrel and idiot, but it does illustrate to some extent the traditional male and female roles in Latin America. Though not all Latin males are "macho" in the pejorative sense of the word, it would be absurd to deny the overall subordination of women to men. In a continent where half the population would be classified as "poor," women are the more miserable and defenseless of this segment. They are less educated and are victims of irresponsible fathers. A very high percentage have children outside of marriage or a stable relationship and when the father leaves, the mother most likely finds the man eluding every obligation to his offspring. Latin American children tend to be "the mother's responsibility."

Of course, this phenomenon is not exclusive to the region; it takes place in any rigidly patriarchal society. (And all societies are patriarchal to some degree, suggests anthropologist Steven Goldberg; he believes biological factors may be responsible, an idea he tries audaciously to document.) For the purposes of this book, the objective is to try to understand the origin and historical evolution of this ancient attitude. By better understanding it, perhaps its worst effects can be alleviated.

GENDER ROLES IN GREECE

If our premise is that the institutions and behaviors of Latin Americans need to be analyzed in a Western context, then the crucial point of departure is Greece — the land of Pericles, Sophocles, Aeschylus, Socrates, Plato, and Aristotle. We could also go back to a more remote point in time and look at how, in primitive cultures, a dominant male led groups of hunters as they roamed through forests and huddled in caves, or how stratification and specialization by gender was reaffirmed with the development of agriculture — the men warred and hunted while the women worked for the harvests and cared for the children; but there is no need to return to such a distant point in history.

Among the Greeks, the founders of democracy and, to a degree, of equality, not all residents of the city-states had rights. Slaves were "objects" to be owned and could be subjected to any form of violence. Women lived in a similar condition. They were practically invisible in the Greeks' *machista* society. They lived secluded in the gynaeceum. As young girls, they learned to sew and sing. Rarely did they venture out onto the street or market, for men did the shopping and the selling. They were allowed to experience only theatrical entertainment — tragedies, mostly, and hardly ever piquant comedies — and the popular feasts dedicated to Dionysus. Not even in Sparta, where they often walked with breasts exposed, did Greek women have many rights.

The great virtue of the young woman, and later of the mature woman, was the *sofrosyne*. With a kind of calm amiability and docility, the ideal woman was supposed to be sensible, unlearned, puppy-like, humble, and have about her an air of chasteness and servility. She married at the age of 15 — and never for love — a man over 20 who had already passed the *efebia*, the two-year military service generally completed after reaching adulthood at 18. The girl's father, brothers, or other family adults, without consulting her, negotiated her marriage and the dowry they were obligated to provide, preferably to a member of the same *fratria* — a young man likely descended from common ancestry. The couple was supposed to add to the family tribe with their children.

No written laws existed against incest, but the literature of the day and popular tradition discouraged sex between siblings and especially sex with one's sons or daughters, citing the wrath of the gods as a possible consequence. Unions between uncles and nieces or between cousins, however, were not as strongly condemned. The purpose of marriage was procreation, to create children and perpetuate the lineage of the family and the *fratria*, thereby providing caretakers for the aged when they were unable to provide for themselves. The Spartans viewed succession as so important that, when a male appeared to be impotent, they sometimes turned to professional "impregnators": virile, robust men ever ready to carry out the task.

Marriage was an oral contract certified before witnesses in a simple ceremony, preferably in winter and under a full moon, in a manner similar to the ceremonies Romans later performed and that Latin Americans carry out today. Much as Catholics appealed to Saint Anthony as their matchmaker, the Greeks had deities to whom they dedicated their marriage and to whose glory the bride dedicated her childhood toys and her most intimate personal belongings.

As part of the rites, at a different place and moment, the bride submitted to a purification ritual in water. Afterward, she joined the banquet celebrated in her father's home where she cut and divided the wedding cake. In separate rooms the men and women ate a good amount of food, generously washed down with wine. Musicians played and sang, their tunes sprinkled with bawdy sexual innuendo. After the feast, the couple climbed onto a cart to take them to the groom's home as the musicians followed behind. When the couple reached the *thalami*, the nuptial chamber, and they received final felicitations, the musicians and friends left them to consummate their union.

Children were for the most part eagerly desired, but when they were not, it was legal to get rid of them. They were the "property" of the father, and if for some reason they were unwanted — almost always because they were female — they were simply abandoned to die of hunger, thirst, or cold in the winter, an infanticide carried out amid society's general indifference. The Spartans, so focused on people's physical traits, were early practitioners of eugenics. They examined the newborn to check for physical defects. If any were present, or seemed likely, they carried the baby to a precipice and hurled it over. They could also sell the infant, who then became a slave forever; or, in the best of cases, give it to a childless couple. The practice of child selling was rather common among poor families.

There were two circumstances under which a husband could divorce his wife: whenever he felt like it, and whenever she committed adultery. In the second instance, he had no choice or he would lose his rights. An Athenian citizen could not simultaneously maintain both his privileges and the shame of having been cuckolded by his woman. He had to choose. In either case, divorce meant having to return her dowry. He divorced her simply by telling her; and then she was left with three options: returning to her family's home, begging, or — if she had the looks and age for it — prostitution. On the other hand, if a Greek woman desired a divorce, she had to appeal to the *arconte*, or magistrate, and list in writing the reasons why she wanted to dissolve the marriage. Often these justices ignored her petitions as typical "female complaints."

The restricted life of a woman contrasted sharply with the life of a man. Greek men could and did share their emotional lives with three types of women: wives (generally confined to the home); *hetairas,* or courtesans who sang and played musical instruments in the many legal brothels; and mistresses, with whom they maintained stable relationships. Socrates apparently felt closer to Mirto than his wife, Jantipa. Likewise, Pericles adored Aspasia, the famous lover he eventually made his wife.

Greek men could also turn to other sources of pleasure, namely adolescent males or boys, whom they actually loved. Given women's negligible importance in Greek society, it appears that only in homosexuality could men find an especially intense and spiritually satisfying relationship. Women were for impregnating; young men were for tender love. This idea was what Plato defended in the *Banquet* and Aeschylus described in the bond between Achilles and Patroclus. It was also perhaps partly responsible for the gallant valor of the Sacred Battalion of Thebes, a military unit formed by homosexual couples. Every man fought fiercely in defense of his cause and lover, an observation that has led more than one historian to see excessive fraternity among soldiers as the origin of this particular relationship. Others prefer to attribute the origin to the close relationship between teachers and their disciples or to the hypocrisy of a society that dictated very severe laws against pederasty (the adult "protector" was the *erasta,* the "protected" youth the *erómeno*), but in reality tolerated it with astonishing ease.

What of women and female homosexuality? It existed, naturally, as Sappho demonstrated with her poetry, written on the isle of Lesbos one century before the splendid golden age of Athens, the fifth century B.C. But such a phallocentric society was too concerned with its own male supremacy to give much importance to what women did in the privacy of the gynaeceum. It was hardly worth legislating against.

GENDER ROLES IN ROME

The Romans, who absorbed so many influences from Athens, granted the family patriarch the same absolute prerogatives as the Greeks had done. However, by the time of the empire, this fierce autonomy had been considerably weakened by a series of laws and decrees protecting those who until then had been mere puppets in the capricious hands of adult males.

For the first time, the hereditary right of illegitimate sons and daughters was recognized. Selling one's children into slavery was prohibited, and the rate of infanticide declined, although the practice was not completely outlawed until several centuries later. Some writers of the time chose to see these developments as the rise of overindulgence toward children. Whereas, before, the father's face had loomed severe and punitive, now it assumed a humane and tolerant expression. Critics found this attitude harmful to the social order.

Naturally, the changes did not occur through any "revolutionary" process but over a slow evolution of attitudes, which many men opposed and writers satirized. These men felt uncomfortable with intellectual women and even worse with athletic women who could hunt and play sports. In any case, women — of little value in Greek society — reached a high prominence in Rome. Their status changed dramatically. They no longer had to submit to marriage *cum manus*, totally subject to the husband's will, but to marriage *sine manus*, which took into account their criteria and feelings, as well as their acceptance of the man. Now there was, or could be, love between a couple, or at least mutual convenience, and the couple could know each other before consenting to a union. Women had emancipated themselves to enjoy a relative equality — or, at least, a higher social status than they had known in Greece.

Though there were many types of marriage ceremonies, the most popular made it to the West and Latin America. It continues to be an agreement made before witnesses, only now before a priest who repeats a speech in which he asks the couple if each freely consents to the union and vows to love and protect the other. Previously, this role was filled by a type of soothsayer, the *auspex*, who foresaw in his arts the good or ill fortune of the pair, formulating his prediction after consulting the entrails of an animal sacrificed in honor of the gods. If the prognosis was favorable, as was almost always the case, the bride dressed accordingly: orange veil, red hairnet, white tunic, and a crown of flowers.

During the ceremony the bride, surrounded by her maidens of honor, exchanged rings with the groom; they placed them on each other's ring finger, to wear from that moment onward. The ceremony culminated with a kiss on the lips. Because of a curious anatomical myth perpetuated by ancient medicine, it was thought that through the ring finger ran a keen "nerve" originating from the heart, which the Romans saw as the seat of love. After the ceremony, men and women shared the table at the banquet (a barrier was now gone), and the musicians as always provided the entertainment. The couple departed amid congratulations, a scene with which we are intimately familiar today.

Once in the bedroom, the Romans adopted other attitudes that we would today describe as chauvinist. Aware of his virility, only the man could initiate sex, and relations with the wife were apparently fairly unimaginative. Still, the same male Romans enjoyed other carnal pleasures generally censured from our present perspective, continuing the Greeks' traditions with slaves or young boys, most often pre-pubescent. The gesture of virility was considered acceptable; the one who submitted was very much viewed as the inferior. Something of this attitude survives in the Latin mentality of our day. Similarly, a woman "attempting to be a man" was viscerally repugnant to the Romans. Perhaps this, too, is one of the roots of today's machismo.

For a society increasingly open — critics would say "corrupt" — it would be natural to think that divorce, as easy for the woman to obtain as the man, would be the order of the day. It required only seven witnesses to the decision and a written communication to the spouse terminating the marriage. Alleging adultery was sufficient cause; it was punishable by law yet was practiced by both sexes commonly. It was also enough to cite "indecorous conduct" and other reasons that today would seem disloyal, such as a partner's old age and illness. Certainly, divorce by mutual consent existed. The woman could own property under laws that protected her. The breakup of a marriage did not necessarily mean instant poverty for her. Sometimes she multiplied her fortunes by immediately pairing up with another, more economically powerful male.

However, to the misfortune of women and despite existing Roman customs in what would soon become Spain — known as *Hispania* and situated on the Roman Empire's western border — the Visigoths who had burst onto the peninsula in the fifth century, imposed rules and behavioral traits closer to what today would be considered "macho." One such trait was the cult of virginity, for which, symbolically, husbands paid a dowry before marriage. Another was the total repression of female adultery, an offense to be avenged with blood (but never masculine blood, as male adultery was accepted without objection). The court of these "barbarians," federated under the Roman Empire, was clearly polygamous.

A society profoundly influenced by military values, the Visigoths practiced dueling to the death for offenses against honor, a savage custom that took hold in the Spanish soul and left a mark still visible a thousand years later in the theater of the Golden Age. They also had numerous brothels, which multiplied in times of scarcity and hunger, and the poor — more the Hispano-Romans than the Visigoths — tended to sell themselves into slavery. According to Saint Isidore of Seville, who subscribed to the rationale of blaming the victim, the fact that certain destitute people were willing to sell themselves into slavery meant that they deserved to be slaves. Not only did the poor use themselves in these transactions, but they also sold their unwanted children. As for the children they did keep, they were considered adults four years earlier than in Roman society. The Visigoths became adults at 14.

Harsh and endogamous, the Visigoths were averse to mixing with the "bland" Hispano-Romans but ultimately had to do so for demographic reasons: they barely numbered 200,000 to about six million Hispano-Romans. They remained inflexible, however, on their stance that slave owners, male or female, could not have sexual relations with their own or another's slaves. The price was torture and death. It was, however, legitimate to cut off a slave's hands or feet, to leave him one-eyed, to castrate him or amputate his penis, and to wrench off his nose, lips, or ears. Slaves did not even "marry" in the free person's sense of the word. Like animals, they formed a *contubernium*, a temporary marriage that the master terminated at will, and to him also went the fruits of these uncertain couples.

In addition to the unfortunates who were constrained to sell themselves out of hunger, prisoners of war were enslaved and for the most part, so were debtors who could not repay what they owed. One of the last laws decreed by the Goths, who were profoundly anti-Semitic, made all Jews in the kingdom slaves. Although it was never implemented, it does explain why Jews received the Muslim invasion as a sort of relief. In general, for the Goths, life had a certain value, and depending on whether one was male or female, young or old, the value differed. For judicial reparation after an assassination, men were worth twice as much as women of the same age. Small children barely had any value. In old age, the "price" for men and women dropped and became the same. The Visigoths were a fierce warrior people. All suffered consequences as a result, but women suffered the most.

CHRISTIANITY, SEX, AND GENDER ROLES

Despite the Barbarian influence, the most profound change in the woman's role in the Western Roman Empire came from the gradual triumph of a Judeo-Christian ethic. Although the gospels preached understanding for women sinners, citing the repentance of Mary Magdalene, from Saint Paul on there appeared a very severe attitude toward "sins of the flesh." The Jew who converted to Christianity on the road to Damascus identified four basic enemies of the soul: prostitution, adultery (of deed and thought), "voluptuous living" (masturbation or hedonistic sexual activity), and homosexuality.

To Saint Paul, in the pursuit and conquest of spiritual perfection sexuality was an inconvenience to be remedied through marriage. The final goal of marriage was not a couple's physical gratification but procreation and strict control of the passions. Marriage was a deterrent against the demon, a "contract" in which sex, always in the proper missionary position, was relegated to a conjugal duty. Much later, Saint Jerome, like John Paul II just before the end of the 20th century, condemned lust within marriage.

For the most fanatical, the Judeo-Christian God was to be placated by sexual abstinence, as well as mortification and the abandonment of material goods. The Church stood adamantly against any expression of sensuality, since passion could only indicate (and encourage) the distraction of attention from serious spiritual matters. Hence, monks' fundamental vows were poverty, chastity, and obedience. This view inspired the anchorites in the desert, cults of flagellants, and cenobites secluded from the world and sometimes voluntarily deprived of speech.

The Catholic Church is fundamentally a masculine structure in which women occupy an auxiliary position. It is an institution of men, and men are tempted by women, who lead them to perdition and hell, or so the logic goes.

A wedding before a priest, as it is understood and enacted today, did not become institutional until the twelfth century, when the ceremony moved from the realm of private life and church ceremony into parish records. The celibacy of priests also did not become obligatory until well into the Middle Ages, and there is consensus that the principal reason behind this practice was to preserve the Church's patrimony by not having to divide tithes among priests' offspring. The chastity of the clergy was debated intensely since all of the apostles save two, Paul and Barnabus, were not only married, but also traveled with their wives as they went about proclaiming the "good news."

Ladies and Gentlemen

In medieval Spain, the Christian view of marriage devoid of sensuality contrasted with what went on in the peninsula's Islamic regions, though there were great commonalities, as well. The Koran allowed polygamy — up to four wives, or however many could be maintained. Without a doubt, this society was designed for the enjoyment of men. Women had to hide their faces behind veils to discourage passions or shield themselves amid the latticework of harems, guarded by (sometimes) inoffensive eunuchs. Female adultery was considered a grave offense, punishable by death. Women were the property of the *macho* who hoarded them. Hitting or verbally abusing them was perfectly acceptable. One Arab proverb states, "When you get home, beat your woman. You won't know why, but she will." Rejecting and discarding women was a simple matter. Islamic religious authority, much like its Christian counterpart, was entirely masculine and generally misogynous. This asymmetry extended to the afterlife, where males who attained glory also enjoyed beautiful women. Even in heaven, Arab women remained mere instruments of male pleasure.

Among medieval Christians, fear of female adultery and its accompanying social dishonor was no less than in the Muslim world. A woman's adultery was always less offensive than the dishonor of not avenging it with her blood.

Between the twelfth and fifteenth centuries, a curious tendency arose to idealize women and this development was reflected in the poetry of the troubadours then appearing in Provence. It was very soon imitated in all the areas where Romantic languages were beginning to flourish. Suddenly, the sinning Eve denounced from the church pulpit became a chaste gentlewoman desired by knights who were determined to perform any deed to win her heart.

Was there in the "revaluation" of noblewomen (peasant women not figuring into chivalry) a diminishing of medieval society's macho views? Absolutely not. Masculine values were at stake: it was all about exhibiting courage and ferocity in combat and delineating areas of patriarchal authority. The maiden was won by an absurd and excessive feat, after which the knight blustered and boasted. In reality, this behavior represented an immature, almost juvenile approach of expressing masculine identity. It was not, as some thought, a type of pro-woman cult, but a narcissistic way to worship men's attributes.

The idealized relations between highborn ladies and wandering knights — tenderly ridiculed by Cervantes in *Don Quixote* a century later — reflected the enormous misogyny spreading through Europe since the late Middle Ages, a sentiment that would culminate with the barbaric holocaust of women carried out at the end of the 16th century. During the so-called "witch hunts," more than 100,000 women were burned in Western Europe. Only some 20 percent of the victims were men. The anger was directed at women. Often, before burning them alive, red-hot steel chains were placed on their arms and their breasts were amputated. Their families were forced to watch, and children were beaten so that they would not forget what happened to the "demonized" women burning before them.

Stereotypes, superstition, and religious tensions all played a part in prompting this monstrosity. The supposed witches, the majority of them women over the age of 50, poor and ignorant, were accused of having ties with the devil.

This climate of terror and sadism against women was facilitated by a series of related historical circumstances. The thirteenth century had brought a wave of repression against heresy, and the Inquisition eliminated the *lex talionis*, a law that had once turned upon the accusers the retribution they had sought if their accusations proved groundless. Now, one could accuse anyone of anything, with impunity. The most brutal torments were used to procure the accused's confession. As a result, fear seized women, prompting repeated cases of mass hysteria in which they heard voices and perceived supernatural apparitions, "signs" that confirmed the persecutors' suspicions.

In the meantime, states were gradually getting stronger, to the detriment of feudal lords. The centralized powers could identify with greater precision and rigor their alleged natural enemies: heretics, Jews, lepers, homosexuals, and witches. The slightest eccentric behavior made one a target for repression, so that even cross-eyed, left-handed, or humpbacked individuals came under suspicion. Women could hardly defend themselves. Their testimonies were taken into little account by invariably masculine tribunals often using the *Malleus maleficarum,* or *The Witches' Hammer,* as their guide. Written by two Dominicans, Kraemer and Sprenger, this perverse manual offered instruction for persecuting the possessed. Also, women were barred from pursuing studies. They were denied apprenticeships in the guilds of specialized workers. Only a few managed to enter artistic careers, and none gained recognition from a male-dominated posterity. Women were underappreciated, supposed inferior and treated accordingly.

Against that backdrop came the 16th century Conquest of America. On the Old Continent, terrible religious wars continued to divide Christian Europe. The sadistic abuse of women was equally prevalent among Catholics and Protestants. Countries such as Spain and Portugal dedicated themselves more fervently to the persecution of heretics, Jews, and deviants than witches, though not exactly as a result of their Catholicism. In a Germany divided between Catholics and Lutherans, for instance, the cruelest witch hunts took place in the Catholic sectors. In Trieste, the Jesuit Peter Binsfeld burned 368 witches in 22 small villages. So many died that a single terrified woman remained in each of two tiny villages to tell the story.

One theological reason may explain why the German Lutherans were somewhat less cruel in persecuting witches than Catholics. The Lutherans' devil was the Fallen Angel, a creature also subject to divine will. Still, it is no easy matter to find the causes for the different behavior among Christians in regard to witches. The facts are both articulate and confusing: the Eastern Orthodox Church proved much less cruel than the Roman Catholic Church, and the Catholics more rigorous than the Protestants, while the northern center of Europe saw this criminal conduct reach its highest level of dementia.

THE SPANISH AND SEX IN AMERICA

This was the sexophobic and racist mindset of the Spanish when they came to American soil. They were accustomed to slavery — much curtailed but still extant in 16th century Europe — to the implacable persecution of those who worshipped different gods, and to subjecting women to brutal treatment. It was the Europe of the Renaissance, of Leonardo and Michelangelo, but also of Torquemada, the sack of Rome, and the burning of witches. It was a Europe that claimed to bow before reason and sought to place Man, with a capital "m," at the center of the universe while simultaneously giving itself over to fanaticism and the merciless destruction of enemies or anyone who dared to be different.

Who were these Spaniards who leapt into the conquest? They were young men, better educated than the average Spanish subject, with little or no military experience. Many were *segundones* — that is, of noble lineage, but second rank — on a quest for fortune, adventure, and pleasure, though they swore they were profoundly Catholic. They seldom traveled with their wives, and exhibited great boldness and a total lack of scruples when interacting with the native Indians, who appeared to them more beasts than people. This approach may explain how little more than 25,000 Spanish who crossed the Atlantic between 1492 and 1567, when all the capitals of Latin America had already been founded, came to dominate a hemisphere with a population of close to 25 million at the time of the discovery — a staggering ratio of one Spaniard per thousand natives.

Spanish patriarchal society met Indian patriarchal society in America. When the whites first beheld Moctezuma, they quickly learned that he had 150 women pregnant at the same time. For the native peoples — even with some differences between the Aztecs and the Incas, or between the Guarani and the Araucanian Indians with relation to the more backward Arawak group — the female also occupied a notably inferior station. They were polygamous societies that even, at least in Mesoamerica, sacrificed female virgins to gain the benevolence of the gods, or hanged women to appease the rain and harvest gods.

It was not odd for Columbus to have abducted 12 Indian women on his first voyage without making the slightest reference to the children he left motherless. It apparently never entered his mind. He took the women with the same casualness one would pluck a pineapple from a tree and store it in the ship's hold to show the king. In his journal, he focused on questions such as whether the women were attractive, lighter or darker than the *Guanches* of the Canary Islands, and if they covered their "shame." But it was not always necessary to use force. The Taino and Siboney Indians surrendered their women willingly. For the majority of the conquistadors who followed in the wake of Columbus, Indian women had been created to service them and give them limitless sex. Indian males reinforced this attitude by giving the Spanish their daughters, sisters, and even their own wives to pacify them. The Guaranis sold their women and children without exhibiting the slightest bit of remorse. They gave Cortés 20 women, among them Malintzin, the famous Malinche (later christened "Marina") who after being passed along through other men acted as his interpreter and lover. It was likely that the Conquistador of Mexico came to feel more comfortable with native women than white ones. It has long been thought that his legitimate wife, Catalina Suárez, known as *la Marcaide*, died under strange circumstances shortly after arriving in Mexico to be reunited with her husband.

There were class and rank considerations in the distribution of Indian women. Indian chiefs relinquished their women to the Spanish leaders to allot along economic and social class lines. The white leaders reserved for themselves those females related to chiefs and gave the less important women to the soldiery. Sometimes the Spanish tired of these gifts and expressed their disdain by hanging a pair of Indian women at the camp entrance. Notwithstanding, the Spanish liked to believe the women preferred them, but this was most likely a banal delusion. Terrified, the Indian women sought safety. They understood that having a child by a Spaniard might bring them certain privileges and tended to soften the men. Some Spaniards lost track of the offspring they created, engaging in a furious procreation that after several generations changed the ethnic composition of the New World. It is no exaggeration to view the conquest as a type of genetic feat. "Majesty," wrote one Spaniard in a document he hoped would show his merits in attaining simony, "through my own efforts, I populated the territory under my charge." Another text, by Bartolomé Conejo, colonizer of Puerto Rico, asked for license to install a brothel, guided by the most Christian of principles: to channel the Spaniards' lust and safeguard the honor and virginity of white women. The priests who accompanied the conquistadors were dismayed by the uncontainable desires of the soldiers, and warned that it was doubly sinful to mate with pagans. As a solution, they baptized the Indian women quickly and in groups, and the couplings continued at a brisk pace.

In addition to their sexual duties, Indian women — just as they had in the pre-Columbian world — performed all types of domestic services and acted as beasts of burden, especially during the long time it took horses, asses, and burros to reproduce. In these regions before the Spanish arrived, neither the wheel nor work animals existed, except for the fragile llama. This "technological leap" — as Mexican essayist José Vasconcelos has stated, possibly with some hyperbole — may be seen as compensating women in some measure for the pain inflicted by the trauma of the conquest.

Prostitution was not unknown among the Indians. The Aztecs counted on a corps of young women to calm the anxieties of their warriors. The Spanish also denounced frequent cases of homosexuality in almost all the cultures they came upon and subjugated. Columbus believed he saw homosexuality among the peaceful Tainos, who blew smoke out of their mouths while breathing in the fumes of burning leaves they called "tobacco." Balboa, in Panama's Darien settlement, set his hunting dogs on some 50 *camayos* (what the Indians called homosexuals), and disgusted afterward, burned the survivors. The Church remained inflexible on many customs that were supposedly found among Incan families. Hernando de Soto took a whole convent of young Incan virgins and distributed them among his soldiers. The Incan nobility — *ñustas*, *coyas*, and *pallas* — had no better fate. Pizarro impregnated the stepsisters of Atahuallpa and Huáscar, the two belligerent heirs to the Incan throne. For the Incan aristocracy, joining with the conquistadors was a way of maintaining privileges. For the conquistadors, the subjugation of the defeated hierarchy was a means of asserting power. The resulting *quid pro quo* was obvious.

From the Spanish perspective, everything led to and justified the subjugation and virtual enslavement of the Indians: their sexual customs, human sacrifices, cannibalism, and pagan idolatry. The Spanish, as all conquerors in history, saw the straw in the other's eye, but not the beam in their own. Setting the dogs on the Indians was not barbaric; it was like hunting hares. Although the Laws of the Indies declared otherwise, the Indians were not, in reality, people. They were brutes, sexually corrupt and dim-witted, to be controlled and educated by the sword.

Tragically, the conquerors' disdain for the conquered ultimately entered the consciousness of the Indian and mestizo population. The extermination and abuse of the natives continued and even increased after the establishment of the republics. The frequent Indian killings went on throughout history at the hands of guerillas, paramilitary troops, and soldiers in countries such as Peru, Guatemala, Brazil, and Mexico. At the beginning of the 16th century, the Queen of Castile decreed that the inhabitants of the New World were vassals of the Crown with full privileges and rights, but no one paid much attention. Quickly, *machismo* took root in the New World, and all of its terrible consequences followed.

5. An Economy Twisted At Birth

It seems that racism, unjust hierarchies born of the conquest, and general disenchantment with the state in Latin America all played a part in impeding economic development. But a deep gulf also emerged from a vision the Spanish transplanted to America that remains today.

An anecdote may help to illustrate the point. Costa Ricans met the 21st century with an intense labor struggle intended to stop the government from relaxing, even moderately, the state monopoly on telephony and electricity services, a step that would have allowed it to partner with large foreign companies bringing in capital and new technology. This opposition to a measure that is indispensable in today's world was widespread and immensely self-destructive.

Without a doubt, the great economic debate in Latin America from the end of the 20th century to the early 21st centers on defining boundaries between public and private domains. Costa Rica's is not an isolated case. Similar struggles have taken place in Colombia, Guatemala, El Salvador, Uruguay, Argentina, and simply all of Latin America. The underlying idea is that the interests of society are always better served by the state than by "greedy" capitalists, a paradoxical view held by societies that simultaneously view the state as an abominable, corrupt, and wasteful administrator.

Furthermore — and here comes the patriotic argument about privatization — the appropriation of public, or state, properties is seen merely as a way of weakening a nation's economic strength. A country is not composed only of a territory, an ethnicity (or several ethnicities), a language (or several languages), a tradition, spiritual ties, a historical memory, a common goal and institutions. To these the Latin American mind feels we must add (for less-than-clear reasons), its electrical plants, communications companies, mines, insurances, some banks, and certain factories, even if they work deficiently. The business in question only has to be able to brand itself with the vaporous qualifier "strategic" and convince society that leaving the company in the hands of irresponsible businessmen would be dangerous. The idea in Stephen Decatur's famous expression, "My country, right or wrong," unfolds in a curious variation: "My national company, efficient or not."

There are other reasons why privatization is opposed. People believe that the cost of services, once in private hands, would surely rise, to the benefit of a few local or foreign businessmen. Latin Americans prefer that the government fix the prices of public services and necessities in a "fair" way — subsidizing them out of the nation's general treasury.

In the Latin American world, there is not enough appreciation for successful businessmen or captains of industry. Any list of the 100 richest men of the country almost always coincides in its entirety with the 100 most hated, who are faulted for the extensive poverty of the nation. The millions of indigent and malnourished citizens are seen as the victims of these unscrupulous millionaires. So says the Left, reinforced from numerous religious pulpits and universities. This argument is the catechism of all populist parties, and in Latin America, almost all political forces, including conservative ones, are populist.

Many of these criticisms are justified, but not for the reasons given by detractors of the free market. What malfunctions in Latin America is not the market or competition, but their absence. What should be censured is the constant collusion between businessmen and the government for influence-peddling and the deceitful award of public contracts. For centuries, Latin American businessmen, with some notable exceptions, have found that economic power gives them political power and the capacity to scheme for greater enrichment. By the same token, government leaders, again with plausible exceptions, have discovered that political power gives them access to economic power, which in turn multiplies their ability to gain more political power. The two complementary corruptions feed each other.

Still, the bitter debate over privatization is part of a greater problem. In truth, Latin Americans have little regard for the market economy. In the previous example, labor unions and numerous consumers opposed privatization in favor of state capitalism, but local producers protest just as loudly when a government crushed by its shortage of resources proposes reforms consisting of opening the market, reducing tariff protection, or ending subsidies. The reasons cited to oppose the privatization, in addition to strictly economic ones (i.e., "the local workers will lose their jobs"), inevitably assume a moral tone: "National industry must be protected from foreign competition." If the poor associate their country with public, or state, companies, the richest manage to present subsidization as another form of patriotism.

Conversely, Latin American leaders have never been more popular than when they have tried to "nationalize" private holdings. It tends to be the most attractive aspect of nearly all successful political programs. A large part of the legend and prestige of Mexico's Lázaro Cárdenas, Argentina's Juan Domingo Perón, Venezuela's Carlos Andrés Pérez (at least during his first tenure), Costa Rica's José Figueres, and Bolivia's Paz Estenssoro is due to their nationalization of foreign-owned property, regardless of the subsequent results. Here, and in the countless attempts at "agrarian reform" intended to break land monopolies, three intense Latin American passions are satisfied: depriving foreigners of their holdings, supposedly enriching the country, and contributing to individuals' economic prosperity. The goal of many Latin American citizens, it seems, is to live off the state, and not for the state to live off them — a norm that, *sensu contrario*, is emblematic of the most developed societies.

Moreover, general perceptions do little to reinforce the concept of economic freedom. If a group of Latin Americans had to say whether prices should be left to the free play of supply and demand or fixed by reputable economists, they would most frequently choose the second option. A similar answer would be provided regarding worker salaries and housing rent prices. Generally, Latin Americans expect economic justice to be imposed from the outside by ethical, conscientious individuals in positions of power and never as the result of the market or agreements freely made. Economic freedom has few followers in the region. Its premises prove contrary to popular intuition.

Apparently, this nationalistic, interventionist, and anti-market mentality, sustained by the great majority of Latin Americans, does not result from an appraisal of the economic realities of the region. What is obvious in Latin America — as opposed to the United States, Canada, Europe, and Japan and other Asian enclaves — is the weakness of the production apparatus. National companies, state- and private-owned, produce little; and what they do produce is generally of very low quality and little added value. At least in the case of state companies, it is done with disregard for the real costs of operation. Distribution methods tend to be inefficient. Management makes no use of modern administrative tools. Banking systems are untrustworthy and the legislation that regulates them poor. Innovation is minimal and originality practically non-existent. All these factors lead to high numbers of unemployed, low salaries, and poor work conditions. Capital is chronically low and a great portion of what could be available instead "leaks" to other countries with clearer laws and better legal guarantees, countries where currency is not devalued from an inflation born of tax collection disorder and public spending.

How can we explain Latin America's divergence from the Western economic model? There are centuries-old ideas that remain entrenched in people's intellectual memory, ultimately shaping beliefs as well as attitudes and behaviors. It is very probable that a rural Bolivian labor unionist or a Paraguayan small businessman has never read a word of Aristotle and knows nothing of the existence of Saint Thomas Aquinas, but their ignorance does not save them from suffering the consequences of these and other powerful thinkers of our heritage. It was Keynes who said we inevitably live under the influence of some obscure economist of the past. He could have added the influence of a theologian or a philosopher. So it is: ideas have consequences, even the most ancient.

THE LIVING PAST

As Murray N. Rothbard explained in his formidable work, *An Austrian Perspective on the History of Economic Thought*, the first economist in history was Hesiod. His didactic poem of the eighth century B.C., *Works and Days* — 828 verses lacking the slightest lyrical emotion — proposed an ethical code to make peasants more honest and efficient. Even though Hesiod's work may have been well known by the Greeks, who used it as a didactic tool, the first truly influential figure in Western thought was Plato. In essence, more than 300 years after Hesiod's poem, halfway between the fourth and fifth centuries B.C., Plato designed his ideal republic. He proposed formulas and measures that began to mold an authoritarian worldview in a model of society where a leader, made legitimate by his intelligence and reason but not necessarily blessed by the consent of the people, ruled from the top down to benefit the masses.

Two of Plato's works, the *Republic* and the *Laws*, are keys to understanding his political-economic thought. To achieve a successful society, Plato proposed an oligarchy headed by a philosopher-king with the help of other thinkers. He thought it risky for common, uneducated people to make important decisions. That function belonged to the state, a state whose guards carried out the basic tasks of strict police control and where property was collectively owned.

Plato was the precursor of the totalitarian state, of fascism and communism. He does not write precisely of political parties, but he does limit rights and authority to 5,000 noble, landowning families. Plato lived in a culture that mythicized the *polis*, the "city praised by all." The *fratrias*, more or less familial lineages, were always inscribed in the *polis*. The cult of the *polis* predates the cult of the modern state. Patriotism was urban, at this point. The city was beloved; poems and odes were devoted to it. It was up to the state to select couples and to officiate at weddings, and also to decide which children would live or die. *Eugenesia*, the Greek word for the selection at birth of the strong and beautiful, best guaranteed the survival of the group. Most likely to the Greeks, *eugenesia* did not seem excessively cruel, for infanticide was accepted and frequently practiced. Nonetheless, the most destructive legacy Plato left to Western tradition was not his call for the totalitarian state but his stigmatization of trade and manual labor. To his aristocratic sensibilities, merchants and craftsmen were offensive — inferior and contemptible beings. Only intellectuals, warriors, priests, and farmers merited respect. The execrable rest, along with slaves and *metecos*, were the lowest form of humanity.

Luckily, Plato's finest disciple at the Academy, Aristotle, departed considerably from his master's thinking. Aristotle distrusted uniformity and celebrated the virtues of diversity. Authority, he believed, should not *descend* from the dome of power but *ascend* from popular will. If Plato was the intellectual father of totalitarian collectivists, Aristotle provided the earliest theoretical defense of democracy and a market economy. Where Plato defended collectivism, Aristotle supported private property, advancing a psychological argument that resonates still: owners of things, proprietors, take much better care of their belongings. Furthermore, it is unjust to give everyone the same goods because those who work less will have no incentive to make a determined effort to increase their output.

Aristotle's intuition was exceptional in economic matters. Private property not only stimulated progress, he believed, it was a natural human tendency. One's work allowed for the accumulation of possessions. When overabundant, these possessions inspired benevolence and philanthropy. Private property made a person better, not worse. People fail to give because they are poor, or live on what they can get and cannot exercise their better virtues. Wealth does not devalue them; it evokes their nobility. Aristotle also discussed the price of goods, and came to the conclusion that the market should best decide price. Value is subjective and depends on the interest buyers and sellers have in a transaction.

Aristotle was the first champion of the market, and his wisdom should be celebrated. Unfortunately, as a good aristocrat, he shared Plato's intense disdain for intermediaries, merchants, and manual laborers. He also failed to grasp the need to charge interest on loans or late debt payments. He thought money should be given in exchange for goods and could not conceive of exchanging it for more money. Interest seemed to go against natural law, and he argued against it on moral grounds. This opinion, resurrected centuries later, would become a heavy weight on the European economy, perhaps even heavier on the Spanish economy. Leading to grave moral reflections, it would become the point on which economics, ethics, and theology converged in an agonizing debate.

Another group of Greeks who appeared after Aristotle, the Stoics, left their mark on Western political-economic thought, although their reflections had little to do with the market. The Stoics endorsed a philosophy globally conceiving of man based on ethics. Their great teacher Zeno of Citium preached in Athens near the *Estoa* gate, thus giving the sect its name. They came to prominence a hundred years after Plato, between the fourth and third centuries B.C., and defended the individual's rights before the state. The person and not the *polis*, or state, they argued, was of the utmost importance, possessing certain rights that preceded the community's. The Athenian was more important than Athens. From this reasoning followed *iusnaturalismo*, the idea that certain natural rights should protect individuals from the wishes and will of the collective. One of those rights, some followers of Stoicism concluded, was the right to own property.

The Stoics were great Roman thinkers and statesmen such as Cicero, Seneca, and Marcus Aurelius. To the Romans, the Greeks were members of a superior culture, and among them, the Stoics were the most respectable, of a strong moral fiber. It was therefore not odd for Cicero — the great writer and famous orator and judge — to defend the idea of natural rights. He died in 43 B.C., shortly before the birth of Jesus, condemned to execution by his political enemies. Nevertheless, Stoicism left an imprint on the subsequent evolution of Christianity. Though the

Romans barely made a mark on economic science, they bequeathed to posterity two institutions that made possible the sustained development of nations: private law, which allowed for free contracting, and mercantile law, which regulated transactions and prevented abuses. Two thousand years later, great specialists of the 20th century, among them Nobel Prize winners James Buchanan and Douglas North, demonstrated the close relationship between legal institutions and economic development.

Unfortunately, the Romans, like the Greeks, were disdainful of commercial activity and manual labor. Their patricians — senators, nobles, and generals — owned great estates and plantations but delegated their management to "inferior" persons, often slaves. The buying and selling of slaves was a principal source of wealth and was done on a scale that the world would not know again until the black trade. The 140,000 residents of the Greek city of Corinth and 30,000 of Taranto, for example, were sold as slaves. One of the greatest material incentives to recruit soldiers was the process of collecting war booty, or capturing human beings and selling them to slave traffickers. The "negotiating" was so extensive that before starting their campaigns, Roman generals settled the price of future captives with slave traders.

Using the traders did not mean liking them, however. German historian Ernst Samhaber explained the Roman attitude by revealing the Latin etymology of the word *comerciante* ("merchant" or "trader"). It is a derivation of *caupo*, a species of scoundrel somewhere between rogue and thief, usually in charge of an inn where he gouges prices and robs his clients and guests. The Roman authorities tended to hold the *caupo* suspect until he demonstrated his unlikely innocence.

Roman law, however, handed down to posterity several important concepts. First, Theodosius II in 434 and then Justinian in 530 (at the time governing from Byzantium) established that a price should be freely agreed to between parties, only adding a provision that spawned multiple misunderstandings: the *laesio enormis*. This provision was made to protect the merchant compelled to part with his goods because of a *force majeure*, an extraordinary circumstance beyond his control. If he had to lower his prices and suffer considerable damage, the circumstance could be referenced at a later date to invalidate contracts.

At this point, another player had entered the scene. After a great struggle, Rome had become Christian. The Church's bishops and priests opined extensively on these worldly subjects, to the extent that, from the fourth to the 17th century, everything that was declared about these topics was almost the exclusive province of the ecclesiastic hierarchy. In effect, the Nicene Council of AD 325 condemned the *turpe lucrum*, adding that if to the Romans the merchant's desire to gain wealth was inelegant and socially undesirable, to the Christians it was worse: it was the sin of greed, deserving of eternal hellfire. *Turpe lucrum* was the term for excessive profit. *Lucrum*, from which the Spanish word *logro*, or "achievement," is derived, was not the honorable businessman's virtuous deed. It was the usurping of that which belonged to another. In the same century, Saint Jerome explained it with transparent ingenuousness: what one gains, the other loses. He felt supported by the New Testament — had not Jesus violently expelled the merchants from the Temple?

The Church did not, however, have a unanimous voice on this issue. A generation after Saint Jerome, Saint Augustine stated the opposite: accept private property and appreciate the merchants. The Old Testament praises work in several instances. It only forbids usury among Jews. Psalm 14 asks, "Lord, who shall enter your Tabernacle?" to which God responds, "He who has not lent money with usury." The New Testament contains passages that seem to criticize the rich, but other sections also recognize their merits. Jewish ethic applauded commercial activity. The early Christian monasteries quickly took to encouraging manual labor and even praising poverty. Many Christians thought God looked with favor on a poor and frugal life. Thus began the fall of the Roman Empire. Augustine died in 430, barbarians besieging Hippo, the North African city of which he was bishop. But this saint, who foresaw the catastrophe, did not attribute the empire's deterioration to the merchants and intermediaries as many then did, and much less to Christianity, as the enemies of the new faith did, but to the uncontrollable depravity of man. It was sin that sank Rome, not necessarily merchants' *turpe lucrum*. Edward Gibbon, the great 18th-century British historian, adopted a rather similar point of view in explaining the fall of the colossal empire.

The next milestone in this matter arose in the Carolingian Empire. Charlemagne forbade usury with dispositions he dictated in Aachen in 789. He also established price controls and regulations on commercial transactions and manufacturing, making the Holy Roman Empire the first great interventionist state of the Middle Ages.

The tight relationship between church and state not only resulted from the monarch's need for validation from the Church, but also from the fact that with the Roman Empire destroyed, the Church had become the age's reservoir of knowledge. Charlemagne, for instance, was barely able to read or write, so that to manage his empire he depended almost entirely on clergymen. He especially relied on the British monk Alcuin. A disciple of English Benedictine Bede the Venerable, Alcuin had been invited to Aachen to organize the Palatine School, the cultural center of the empire that served as a model for the teaching carried out at religious institutions and the scholastic work performed in monasteries, where friars preserved the few libraries then in existence. Thus, the first universities were formed under the auspices of the Church as a logical evolution of episcopal schools run by the different religious orders. The Church had both the authority to fund them and the manpower to run them.

Because the Church created almost all the universities in Europe — Salerno (in the eleventh century), Oxford (1170), Paris (1200), Salamanca and Cambridge (1230) — the great moral themes of religious interest were the focus of a medieval university education, including disquisitions on the fair price of goods, money-lending, and the role and moral nature of merchants. University scholars studied economy insofar as these topics related to theology. After all, several popes — Alexander III, Innocent II, and above all Gregory IX — were jurists who provided almost sacred opinions in economic and legal affairs, which were linked inevitably to theology. Urban III repeated Luke's words: "Give freely, expecting nothing in return." A great expert on moral questions, Urban III doubtless knew very little about the creation and loss of capital.

In the thirteenth century, and decidedly in the fourteenth, France grew into a major European power. The University of Paris became the educational heart of Western Europe. There, German Albertus Magnus met his disciple, Thomas Aquinas (called in his lifetime *doctor angelicus*, or "angelic doctor"), and between them they began to rescue Aristotelian thought. They assumed Aristotle's point of view on economic matters. Financial benefits from commercial transactions were legitimate because merchants ran certain risks. Every transaction carried with it uncertainty. One could lose, *ergo*, it was morally justifiable to reward with earnings those prepared to face that danger. The fair price, as Aristotle proposed, was what the market determined, making it ethically acceptable to have access to private property. However, charging interests for loans was still usury, and Christian morality did not allow it.

Once again the Church collided with usury. Its most learned thinkers did not understand how time could also be an economic factor of primary importance. Saint Bernardine of Siena shed light on the issue. Bernardine, a Franciscan who led a frugal life, was a great preacher and the vicar general of his order. He introduced a "dangerous" novelty — the concept of *lucro cesante*. According to this principle, time during which money is immobilized is a loss to its owner, who cannot then use it for other activities to yield benefits. Bernardine's work, *On Contracts and Usury*, is a clear defense of merchants, the market, and the right to charge interest. The debate had finally moved forward.

Spain in the 16th century, amid the conquest and colonization of America, was the European country with the clearest manifestation of a "pro-market economic tendency," arising from the so-called School of Salamanca, although the universities at Alcalá and Coimbra (in Portugal), the latter under Basque Martín de Azpilcueta, also developed similar concepts. Azpilcueta, theologian and jurist, counselor to popes and confessor to kings, could be considered Spain's first modern economist. In his works, *Comentario resolutorio de cambios* (*A Resolute Commentary on Changes*) and *Comentario resolutorio de usuras* (*A Resolute*

Commentary on Usuries), he clarified for the first time the relationship between price levels and the sum of money in circulation — the origin of monetarism — while explaining with total objectivity the reasons for charging interest on loans.

The School of Salamanca of the 16th century — an early expression of liberalism, an idea the economists of the Austrian School conceded in the 19th century — was the same to which belonged Francisco de Vitoria and Domingo de Soto (both of whom witnessed the debate between Las Casas and Sepúlveda) and later Tomás Mercado, author of *Tratos y contratos de mercaderes* (*Dealings and Contracts of Merchants*), and two Jesuits who had an extraordinary importance in Europe, Francisco Suárez and his contemporary, Juan de Mariana. Suárez, an erudite theologian and jurist who became known, along with Vitoria, as the father of international law for his works on *jus gentium*, also delved into economic science in defense of the market. Juan de Mariana was much more explicit and impassioned, opposing vehemently (as was his nature) state intervention in economic matters. With excellent judgment, he accused the king of causing inflation and currency devaluation through excessive public spending, thereby impoverishing the Spanish. He agreed with Suárez on the legitimacy of tyrannicide as the last resort to protect popular will should a despot forget his duty to law and religion. Small wonder the Inquisition had him jailed and his books listed on the *Index* for years.

It is worth specifying that at the time Mariana declared the "right of tyrannicide" in his 1599 book, *The King and the Education of the King*, the issue was not exactly an abstract debate. Given the climate of violence unleashed by the religious wars between Protestants and Catholics, it was an opinion that could almost be classified as incendiary.

The Spanish King Philip II was an intransigent Catholic; despite the bloody killing of Calvinists four years earlier (on Saint Bartholomew night, August 24, 1572), he took a very dim view of the concessions France made to the (Protestant) Huguenots in 1576. In December 1588, his neighbor the French King Henry III was assassinated by Jacques Clément, a radical Catholic monk who today would be called a

fundamentalist. Henry's successor, Henry IV, was of Huguenot origin —
and it was during his wedding feast in Paris that the massacre of the
Calvinists had taken place. Still, he renounced his Protestantism,
sardonically noting that "Paris is well worth a mass." Nevertheless, in
1610, after forging alliances with German and Swiss Protestants, Henry
IV was stabbed to death by Catholic zealot François Ravaillac, a killing
apparently ordered by the Spaniards and Austrians, although the killer
never confessed to that during the horrible tortures to which he was
submitted. He never admitted having read the writings of Father
Mariana, either, despite his interrogators' insistent questions about the
Jesuit's work and whether he had been motivated by it.

THE INEFFECTIVE AND MISSING TOOLS OF DEVELOPMENT

During the period of the conquest and colonization, there were
many men in Spain who could understand, even if superficially, what
constituted good government for the economy, but their voices did not
reach the monarch or his circle of advisors. The truth is that the Spanish
treasury was suffering a deep fiscal and monetary crisis while first
Charles V, and later his son Philip II, embarked on costly wars. This
expensive habit ruined Spain for centuries, even as the country was
experiencing a political and military boom.

As his German moneylender Fugger said, Charles V may have
understood military matters, but he did not know how to count. Double-
entry bookkeeping had been invented by the cautious bankers of Genoa
in the mid-fourteenth century, and a century and a half later, in 1494, the
Venetian Luca Pacioli, a Franciscan mathematician and friend of
Leonardo da Vinci (who illustrated one of his works), published *Summa de
Arithmetica, Geometria, Proportioni et Proportionalita et Arte Maggiore*, with a
chapter on accounting afterward published as *Tractatus particularis de
computis et scripturis*. These extraordinary innovations were a major
advance in financial practices but, unwilling to sully themselves with
sordid money matters, the people around the king only saw that an

endless flow of gold and silver was pouring in; they could not imagine, much less calculate, that the overall trend was negative.

Apparently, the government was simply incapable of (or uninterested in) calculating budgets. As Spain was gaining stature in the world, it needed an accounting system to estimate costs, specify fiscal expenditures, price assets, ascertain which routes were best for production, and make long-term plans. Yet, none of this figured into the disorganized Spanish government.

It is true that the Catholic monarchs, Charles V's grandparents, had created the *Sala de los Contadores Mayores de los libros de la Hacienda y Patrimonio Real*, or the "Hall of the Senior Accountants of the Royal Treasury and Patrimony" in 1480. It was also true that Barcelona housed Spain's first bank (*Taula di Canvi*) as early as 1401 (although it failed soon afterward) and that in Valencia, merchants understood these issues much better than in Castile. Nonetheless, prior to and during the Renaissance, Spain did not master the financial techniques of the age.

The knowledgeable money managers were foreigners and local minorities. The Genoese had been known for their banking expertise since the twelfth century, and Germans also gained a reputation as bankers. In Spain, financial managers were often Jews or converts to Christianity. As a result, the country lost necessary human capital when it expelled the Jews in 1492. Thousands of merchants and experts in financial transactions exited the country. Those who stayed, becoming converts or *"new Christians,"* lived under the implacable vigilance of the Inquisition, eternally suspicious of those performing the "work of Jews" — an attitude exacerbated by the popular negative perception of financial transactions. Gentlemen and *old Christians* did not enter into dirty jobs connected to money or manual labor. These things were reserved for *la gentuza*, the rabble. This attitude was enormously detrimental to Spain's great enterprise in America and its destiny as a European power and is one of the main reasons why Spain was sinking economically.

Spain's poor economic vision soon manifested itself in a turn of events that disconcerted the monarchs and that even today, 500 years later, inspires grave discussions. Despite the shiploads of silver and gold transferred from America's mines to Spain, the country underwent five economic collapses in 1595, 1607, 1627, 1647, and 1656, dragging down the great financial centers of the day. No one knew — or seriously asked — how much it really cost to arm a fleet, to transport thousands of migrants to New Spain (Mexico) or Potosí (Bolivia), to build towns and roads 4,000 meters above sea level, to raise great religious temples to accommodate the spiritual needs of conquerors and conquered, and to maintain thousands of Indians or black semi-slaves extracting minerals. No one could calculate the cost of constructing cities to control these operations and house the natives vanquished in interminable wars and skirmishes, of equipping ports and strategic crossroads with well-provisioned military installations to prevent sacking by pirates and corsairs, and of escorting the metals to Spain with armed ships. Exhausted by endless war, the kings did not stop to count. In fact, they did not know how.

However, the ruling vision in the metropolis was very clear: the role of the colonies was to enrich the state that possessed them. They were to generate income. The relationship between the dominant powers and their vassal territories had always been understood this way. For all of the Crown's talk that the Indies were part of Castile, in truth, the colonies were more like medieval satellite states forced to pay tribute. (The final decision for an attack on Granada was made when the Moorish ruler refused to continue paying the tribute imposed by the Catholic monarchs.) With the aim of exploiting the new territories to its benefit, Spain planted its banner after each discovery and paraded its soldiers to secure its sovereignty. England, Holland, and France had the same vision.

What went wrong? The empire was the victim of a costly intellectual error born of faulty reasoning. Some people were rich, because they had money, meaning coins — gold, silver, and the cheapest, copper — with their value set in relation to the weight and purity of the metal. No one knew how much it had cost Spain to obtain the metals, bring them back home, and mint the currency — and no one asked. The important thing was to have them. They were necessary to repay the loans taken out to finance the interminable wars. The armies were almost all mercenary forces that demanded, under threat of mutiny, a good wage and some of the spoils from the sacked cities. When these were not forthcoming, they reacted with ferocity. Coins were also useful for importing goods that the Spanish did not produce in the same quality as outsiders: fine cloth, weapons, jewels, clocks, and certain machinery from the north of Europe, Italy, and, increasingly, France. This led to the greatest of paradoxes: Spain was bled dry in an effort to acquire the metals that ultimately served to strengthen her neighbors and sometimes even her enemies.

There is a particular irony to this. A long tradition of currency existed on the peninsula. In essence, the first people to introduce coins to Iberia were Greeks and Carthaginians, with their *drachmas*, *oboli*, and *calcos*. The Romans brought the *denario* — from which we get the Spanish word for money *dinero* — and created royal mints to coin metal. The Goths in the fifth century continued the practice but reduced the quality of the metal. When the Arabs conquered the peninsula in the eighth century, they imposed the *dinar*, which also recalls the Latin *denario*. Under Arab influence, Christians in Spain named their most popular currency with a word taken from their enemies, the Almoravides: *maravedi*. This detail may very well have had some bearing on Christians' ambiguous attitude toward money, although it is hard to say. Certainly, upon the arrival of metal and coins in sixteenth-century Spain, prices quadrupled, confirming Azpilcueta's observation that with a greater number of coins in circulation and the same number of available goods, prices would rise. This was, in a word, inflation. It was followed by deflation when American mines started to run dry. In response, the Crown re-minted coins, artificially multiplying their value and generating a chaos in the economy that provoked starvation in various regions of Spain, which was also struck by plague at the end of the 16th century.

The Catalonians and Valencians, who possessed a sound currency system, emerged relatively unscathed. It was not until the 19th century that Spain adopted a uniform coin for the entire country.

In America, the mines could not yield enough gold, silver, or other metals to solve the chronic scarcity of money. Only cities actually used money; rural areas continued to get by through barter. The ships on which the metal ingots or minted coins were exported to Europe were perpetually attacked by pirates.

The first American to mint coins was Hernán Cortés. There were never enough coins, however, which hindered commerce significantly. Mining required an enormous mass of labor, which was extracted from the Indians. At one point, the mine at Potosí was using the largest number of workers at any company in the world: 13,500 miners and helpers labored through extremely long workdays. Unsurprisingly, it provided half the global production of silver, especially after 1552, when Bartolomé Medina discovered the amalgamation of mercury and facilitated the industrial process. Not even in the mines could workers be paid with coins; instead, they often received a small portion of the mineral they extracted, known as *pepena*.

Because currency was unavailable, gold and silver were weighed, or *pesado*, and a value assigned to it. This gave us the word *peso* — from the gold and silver peso. In 1525, 4.6 grams of gold of 22 karats equaled one gold peso, also known as a *castellano*, exchangeable for 450 maravedi. That was almost the two-month salary of a farmhand. One American-minted silver peso, a highly valued coin, was equivalent to a month's salary of 275 maravedi. Few were in circulation in America; they were in great demand in Europe. The Americans complained about the scarcity of coins, but the Crown paid them little attention, its own problems seeming infinitely more pressing than rumors of aggrieved subjects so far removed.

While the monetary chaos was considerable, the system of fiscal collection and the ways in which the state entered into and incurred its obligations were not much better. It was no coincidence that a large portion of the population joined the convents or the secular clergy, while almost all aspired to form a part of the nobility — neither the clergy nor the nobles paid taxes in Spain or America.

Apart from the shipments from America, the national coffers were replenished by taxes on commerce. There were transportation taxes and customs duties (*almojarifazgo*), especially on the trading of wool. There was also the *alcabala*, a tariff on direct sales and bartering, and the *avería*, a special tax to pay for safeguarding fleets. The latter was similar to the *cruzada*, a papal tax intended to subsidize the wars against the Turks. In general, the Church played a small part in helping Spain with its expenses. The Inquisition contributed the confiscated goods of the condemned, but it was hardly flush with money since it had to fund its own operations. Rome also shared with the state the yield from the sale of indulgences. When this revenue failed to cover costs, the state turned to *juros*, a kind of public debt incurred by the Crown. The *juros* had originated in the twelfth and thirteenth centuries but with the arrival of the Catholic kings, the debt multiplied exponentially. That in itself fueled inflation. There came a moment when Philip II, then the most powerful monarch on earth, ruler of an ever greater empire, feared he would not be able to cover the expenses of his own palace. Between them, he and his father destroyed the German banker Fugger's fortune, possibly the largest in Europe at the time, and in the process also scandalously stripped the Crown of its wealth.

Spain and America certainly formed a powerful union, to which were added the European possessions of the Spanish king. The *tercios*, soldiers of a Spanish military force staffed largely with mercenaries of different lands, were known to be fierce. But this martial strength was no match for the economic strength, or for the skill and refinement of financial management in other parts of Europe. In the north, German cities and the Low Countries had engaged in commerce energetically since the fourteenth century. In their best period, 72 German cities constituted the Hanseatic League, spanning the north of Europe from Flanders eastward as far as Russia. The Baltic and North Seas became its *mare nostrum*, and some years as many as 1,000 ships sailed it in all directions. A remote ancestor of the European Union, the league was formed for trade and the protection of participating countries' maritime lines. Attacking one country led to forced isolation from the rest. The Danes were eventually subdued and Scandinavia joined this commercial world — the same Vikings who had terrorized the rest of Europe in previous centuries. Furs, herring, silk, and wood traveled from one port to another. England and Holland participated in the commerce sporadically, but neither could avoid conflicts and clashes of interests.

In northern Europe — from a scientific, industrial, and financial perspective — a more complex society began to take shape among these Anglo-Germanic peoples. The League gradually decayed, like any political-economic structure, but it left a permanent imprint. The English, Scandinavians, Germans, Dutch, Belgians, and French, while never ceasing their intermittent struggles, had forged a common cultural and commercial space with very similar characteristics as a result of their multiple transactions at different levels. Sixteenth-century Europe had two hegemonic cultural and financial poles in certain cities in northern Italy and northern Europe. Gradually, the gravitational center of civilization shifted to the northern sector of the continent. Spain was a mighty power, but it was eccentric, backward, and outstanding only militarily. Spanish and Portuguese America inherited this marginal position. It could not have been otherwise.

Capital, like life, desperately seeks multiplication. In this corner of the world it was no different. Bruges, the old Flemish city in today's Belgium, became a favorite meeting place for German and Italian businessmen; the House of the Genoese was then still in existence. These bankers and businessmen began traveling and settling in different parts of Europe. They used letters of credit and bills of exchange (which the Genoese had employed for 200 years) instead of coins, and this enabled them to expand commerce tremendously. In the fourteenth century, commercial travelers met in an inn kept by a family named *Bourse* and exchanged documents of credit. Business conducted in good faith became key elements of progress. Indeed, the Spanish words *fe* ("faith") and *fiar* ("to trust" or "to sell on credit") have common etymological roots. Trust became the cornerstone of economic development. Yet, there were few Spaniards among these international businessmen. The culture of trust did not extend to Spain and later America with the solidity it did in northern Europe. "Bourse" was used eventually to christen a plaza and also to identify something more transcendent: the stock exchange, called *bolsa* in Spanish and *bourse* in French. Based on bills of exchange, this market gave rise to companies owned through stock and to the sale of stocks. The first joint-stock companies sprang up in sixteenth-century London. Very soon, Antwerp, Lyon, and Amsterdam also became important financial centers. Entrepreneurs from this region of the world knew how to "move" their capital, and sometimes risked it by speculating on the future harvest of crops.

In the 17th century, Londoners were already using the expressions *bull market* and *bear market* to indicate movement toward an increase in stock value or toward its decline. (No one knows the exact origin of these terms or who used them first.) At this point, various types of players were engaged in speculative activities. In addition to buyers and sellers, there were brokers and there were notaries, who managed the legal jargon needed to protect transactions. This last group, however, did not manage to significantly impede swindling, nor could they stop the gradual proliferation and refinement of legislation intended to address the conceptual complications emerging from these new economic entities. Capitalism, by nature, is about money, but its foundation is legal. Capitalism has two important characteristics: risks associated with the market and security afforded by law. Capitalism cannot exist without legal guarantees and respect for contracts. Modern expressions such as "financial bubble" and "speculative bubble," so decidedly frightening in the 21st century, began in the so-called *Bubble Act* of the 18th century, enacted to clarify ambiguous notary documents.

With the innovations of the capital market, a new way to accumulate wealth and multiply investments, as well as an impersonal way to manage business, had been born. Matters had gone beyond the whims of an individual businessman or his family. The business manager now had to account to shareholders. That pressure contributed to the transparency of commercial activity and forced its efficiency. Anyone wishing to compete for someone else's savings had to guarantee excellence.

Still, all this economic progress moved at a snail's pace in Spain and its colonial possessions. Paper currency — an English or Anglo-French invention introduced by Scotsman John Law, a financial genius working for France at the start of the 17th century and the father of modern credit — was not used widely in Spain until a century later. It is true that Law's experiment proved to be another less-than-trustworthy economic model and ended in collapse, with Law hiding out in Italy and France in the middle of a recession. But his best ideas gave commerce a tremendous boost and changed the face of the West.

After the creation of paper money and the introduction of new ways to extend credit, northern and central Europe separated even further as the number and volume of commercial transactions increased. Capital began to be tested on a new financial engine that allowed its multiplication in a manner never before seen.

What about America? While Spain made relatively poor use of the economic tools of development in the colonization process, the other side of the Atlantic suffered the worsening of problems today we would classify as "structural." The accumulation of capital was not the result of industry, commerce, or the increase of production, but of the distribution of land, war booty, slave labor, and privileges assigned by the Crown. Perhaps the primary source of capital accumulation — a fact that still holds true — was the ownership of land. Originally, land in the colonies was the Crown's property, and was conceded as a favor to its most loyal Spanish conquistadors. The infantry, or *peones* who had fought on foot, received *peonías*, while *caballeros*, or knights, were given *caballerías*. A caballería was more than 40 hectares, the size of six peonías. Large land monopolies arose almost immediately, which often could not be used to their capacity.

What was the meaning of amassing all this useless land? Among the Spanish, the ownership of vast lands was synonymous with social distinction and noble origin. The Crown was eager for agricultural development and therefore sent expeditions of laborers and peasants, even covering transportation and settlement costs. But no sooner did the farmers reach the New World than they abandoned working the land to exploit Indians and blacks, for manual labor was a symbol of inferiority. This view persisted, although toward the end of the 18th century Charles

III officially removed the stigma. Still, it proved difficult for a pragmatic royal decree to banish, in one fell swoop, a view that had held sway for a millennium.

The Church also turned into a prodigious landowner, always with a secure investment in real estate. Everyone wanted land: it did not always generate much income but was always there. Land was the ultimate inheritance. An industry could go bankrupt. Commerce was subject to monetary and financial risk. Land, on the other hand, endured, increasing in value slowly but surely as the population grew, and cities and towns expanded over the countryside. In time, the Church became the largest landowner in America, a fact that did not make the Spanish monarchs happy since the "priests" paid no taxes and often turned their immense properties into fallow lands not cultivated for agriculture. (Hence the curious Castilian term used in the 19th century, after the Crown expropriated the Church's lands: *desamortización*. Society had taken these assets out of the realm of the dead to return them to a life of productivity.)

The Spanish colonial model left its mark on Latin America's business mentality. The equation "land = lineage" is still in force in all Latin American nations today. Being a landowner confers the sense of an old patriarchal and patriotic prestige. Sadly, the conservative tradition of maintaining capital securely invested in land without running the risks of industry and commerce is also still alive. The hope is to increase the investment through the accrued value on the property. As a result, for centuries Latin America saw economies of little vitality — backward, barely competitive, subsisting by exporting raw materials in a world that was gradually building toward an industrial revolution that would peak in England in the 18th century.

Commerce was not a priority for Spain in Europe, and was even less so in the America it had conquered. The mercantilist mindset of the period believed that the role of colonies was to serve as captive markets serving producers in the metropolis, that is, the center of the empire. Latin Americans were not supposed to produce what the mother country did; they were supposed to buy such products. Competition — the key to development — was deliberately thwarted. The economy had to be "complementary." That meant that colonists were to trade only with Spain; they were not to purchase from foreigners, even if the price and quality of goods were better, or sell to them. Commerce had to take place on ships bearing the Spanish insignia, and only in ports chosen by the Crown, such as Cádiz and Seville, initially, with companies formed by royal privilege to enrich specific nobles designated by the monarch in a monopolistic system. This was the "colonial pact."

Naturally, it was undermined at times through contraband dealings with English, French, and Dutch merchants who risked their lives to buy and sell merchandise outside the official channels. When they were caught, they were hanged; but the executions happened infrequently since a prevailing attitude of complicity tended to protect them. Everyone benefited from their activity except the colonial authorities which, having lost a fragment of their ill-served clientele, perpetually awaited the unhurried fleets from Spain. The ships sailed to diverse points, Havana being the first and last great stop, to load and unload "materials" with which to feed the commerce between motherland and colonies. Each run took from two to four months, if and when storms did not sink the vessels or corsairs and pirates did not sack them. This is an eternity, to our modern sense of time, but it was a reasonable period for that civilization of slow consumption, learned patience and a certain kind of fatalism.

Industrial development was not much helped, but it was not always hindered by imperialist designs. According to historian Lutgardo García Fuentes, Spain clearly advanced industrial production in America in at least three sectors (outside of mining): the *obrajes* of textile manufacturing, developed by Aztecs, Mayas, and Incas before the Spanish arrived; sugar harvesting, an ideal crop and industry for tropical and sub-tropical climates, worked by black slaves; and shipbuilding, facilitated by the availability of immense forests. Of the three activities, textile production perhaps reached the highest grade of capitalist development, especially in Mexico. This industry drove the production of other related goods such as fabric dyes, including dyes taken from the indigo plant to give fabrics a blue tint; from logwood to produce a garnet color; and from the cochineal, a tiny insect that lived in the prickly pear and created a practically indelible red substance.

Ranching was another lucrative activity. Horses, swine, and cattle multiplied and adapted well to the vast new territory because natural predators were not numerous. Sheep acclimated to colder zones, multiplying so greatly in Mexico that owners imitated the Castilian *Mesta*, the group that had organized nomadic shepherds over distant lands. But neither ecological niches nor markets tend to benefit everyone equally, and the reproductive success of these animals threatened ruin for the Indians (as it had for Castilian farmers in the Middle Ages) as the proliferating animals destroyed their crops. One curious case — quite revealing of the complexities of the Counter Reformation's religious conscience — involved the mule. It was valued for its strength and was common in Latin America. However, because the mule was a hybrid creature (the offspring of horse and ass) and generally sterile, the authorities discouraged breeding them for obscure theological reasons. They seemed to think something sinful and unnatural existed in this tenacious animal of uncertain conception so beloved by soldiers and farmers.

THE FUNDAMENTALS OF DISASTER

At the close of the 18th century, prominent thinkers in Europe began asking for an end to mercantilism, as historian Carlos Rodríguez Braun related brilliantly in *La cuestión colonial y la economía clasica* (*The Colonial Question and the Classic Economy*). It was not only a matter of an unjust relationship to the detriment of the colonies, but of a paradox: the motherland and the colonies were harming each other. How much did it cost Spain to maintain the colony as a closed shop for a few privileged businessmen? The costly military garrisons and immense bureaucracy appeared to benefit a very minute minority. Adam Smith, referring to the English colonies in America (considerably freer than Spanish and Portuguese territories), wrote, "To protect the interests of a small group of people, society as a whole is harmed." Smith asked for total freedom in economic transactions. To the author of *The Wealth of Nations*, published in 1776 (the same year the English colonies in America began their quest for independence), monopolies prevented the formation of capital, which was the basic element of development. Only the continual growth of capital allowed societies to gain wealth. Smith was not the first English thinker to reject the mercantilist model. In 1760, a clergyman with the English church Josiah Tucker, Dean of Gloucester, was more daring. He defended the idea of independence for the 13 trans-Atlantic colonies, believing it would be beneficial to England. Father Raynal made a similar proposition ten years later in a book verbosely titled *A Philosophical and Political History of the Settlements and Commerce of Europeans in the Two Indias.*

Spain was not immune to this debate. With the 18th century the Bourbons entered into the history of the peninsula and that translated into a constant effort to modernize public administration, until that moment taking as its model the French bureaucracy. Slowly, new liberal, anti-mercantilist ideas began penetrating the ideological body of the ruling class, finally prevailing during the reigns of Charles III and Charles IV, the period in which Spain opened its ports to Latin America, lowered tariffs, and permitted trade with other nations. In this period, the *librecambistas*, or proponents of free trade, managed to put an end to many commercial monopolies. Suddenly, as they had foreseen, economic activity exploded.

It was the era of the great Spanish Enlightenment, boasting thinkers such as Campomanes, Floridablanca, and Jovellanos. However, the changes had come late. At the outset of the 19th century, the Creoles felt they had been wickedly exploited and excluded by the metropolis, blaming Spain, its economic mindset, commercial habits, and unfair legislation for the backwardness of their region. Spanish economist, Álvaro Flórez Estrada, was able to see things from the victim's perspective. In 1811, with rebellious meetings already taking place in America, he published *An Impartial Examination of America's Dissension With Spain.* He did not mince words, proposing free trade and categorically rejecting monopolies. Estrada knew that relations between Spain and

America could not continue under the traditional "colonial pact" structure. The new capitalistic model of economy required that both parties benefit from business. In England a short time later, Jeremy Bentham recommended to the French that they abandon the exploitation of their conquered territories and added a moral argument: a great distance between citizens and the seat of power turns into bad government. He who governs should be close to the governed, who must assume the role of judge and watchdog.

When the Latin American colonies became new republics, they inherited an economic legacy characterized by an aristocratic attitude wherein the upper classes despised commercial and industrial activities. They inherited an antiquated approach to financial management, a system of land tenancy that impeded industrial investment, a production system that was robbed of new techniques that foreign influences would have provided, and a chronic lack of investment capital. Consequently, great numbers of extremely poor people found themselves trapped in an economic system that lacked sufficient flexibility to foster development. All problems are surmountable with time — if and when the causes that create them and the formulas needed to solve them are understood, which does not seem to have been the case here. If we return to the beginning of this chapter and review the Costa Rica anecdote, we would be able to witness the power of the past. There it is, alive and kicking — mercantilist thought that is distrustful of economic freedom and inherently contrary to progress. Curiously, in Latin America today its staunchest advocates are no longer the oligarchs who once benefited from it, but rather, the poor who suffer the most because of it.

6. "LET OTHER PEOPLE DO THE INVENTING!"

If an extraterrestrial were to fly today over the commercial districts of Caracas, Santiago de Chile, Buenos Aires, Bogotá and Quito, it could easily come to the conclusion that these capital cities sheltered forms of civilization and levels of industrial and scientific development comparable with London, Amsterdam, or Los Angeles. Should its hypothetical journey include the central campus of the Autonomous University of México with its student body of 250,000, the world's largest, or the populous University of San Marcos in Lima or the University of Santo Domingo, and should it hear that all three institutions were founded more than 400 years ago, a century before Harvard, it might suppose that Latin America formed part of the planet's intellectual center. Superficial evidence would certainly point in that direction.

The appearance would be misleading. It is true that Latin America does not lack enormous educational institutions and that eminent professionals, experts, and scholars are abundant. However, it is also true that Ibero-America — Spain and Portugal included in this sad assertion — is the cultural pocket that has contributed least to the intellectual development of the West in the last few centuries, an observation that has inspired more than a few insults, such as Giovanni Papini's cruel qualifier, "the stupid continent." What has kept it from the table, where creativity and advancement meet? The reasons are intricate and have fueled major debates over the centuries. The controversy over the existence of "Spanish science," for example, acrimoniously divided intellectuals in the time of Menéndez Pelayo. The arguments have often confused objective fact with emotion, and desires with a misconceived patriotism, as if pointing out deficiencies or weaknesses were a cunning way to sully the honor of the tribe.

Nonetheless, few matters are as important as this one. Why was Spain — and consequently the world she mothered across the sea — never a scientifically and technically innovative nation? Lewis Mumford concluded his famous essay *Technics and Civilization* (one of the century's most impassioned studies of historical sociology) with an appendix listing the 506 inventions, discoveries, innovations, and institutions that changed the face of the earth between the tenth century and 1933, the date of the first edition. On the list only one Spaniard appears, Blasco de Garay, who in the 16th century had the idea of adding paddle wheels to ships, something akin to crossing ships with watermills. Mumford, whom no one can accuse of Anglophilia, missed the histologist Santiago Ramon y Cajal, deserving winner of the 1906 Nobel Prize in physiology and medicine, and Juan de la Cierva, the apt engineer who in 1923 designed the autogyro, a prototype of the helicopter. Also, had he updated the list to the present, he would have included Severo Ochoa, one of the most important genetics researchers. In any case, these few eminent names, plus the Cuban Carlos J. Finlay and the Argentines B.A. Houssay and René Favaloro, do not alter substantially the obvious fact: the contributions of Hispanic people to the Western culture of science and technology has been minimal. In the sphere of the arts, the situation is otherwise; there, the Spanish and Latin American presence is impressive.

At the beginning of the 20th century, when Miguel de Unamuno was confronted with this phenomenon, he dismissed it with the well-known words, "Let other people do the inventing!" He made no attempt to deny the backwardness, as Menéndez Pelayo had tried to do a generation earlier, and instead coined this disdainful phrase as if scientific or technical sterility would have dire consequences. In that, the famous writer was mistaken. Lagging behind in these areas brought the twin disadvantages of severe economic damage and inevitable subordination to other nations. Spain and Latin America became nothing but appendages to the societies that were developing communications, aeronautics, pharmacology, television, biogenetics, the space race, nuclear energy, information technology, and the other disciplines that have characterized the West. Quite simply, adopting these advances passively rather than actively participating in their development meant that the whole civilization — the Ibero-American perimeter, for lack of a better term — had to take on, in a state of subordination, the political and intellectual contour of the more creative nations.

This deficiency has a profound economic impact. The development and propagation of each scientific and technical milestone — in fields such as telecommunications, aviation, electric energy, etc. — increase the aggregate value of the society that produces it. The resulting gap, a widening chasm, is not then a matter of the more powerful states withholding their resources from the poorer ones, as some have claimed. That problem occurred precisely in the pre-scientific age. Rather, the innovative and audacious peoples create more wealth, accelerating their rate of development. Angus Maddison expresses this quite clearly at the beginning of *Dynamic Forces in Capitalist Development* published in 1991. "Since 1820, the advanced capitalist countries have increased their total production seventy times, and today represent half the world's GNP. Their per capita income is today 14 times higher than in 1820 and six times the average corresponding to the rest of the world."

Perhaps the person who best explained the relationship between prosperity and scientific and technical progress was Austrian economist Joseph Schumpeter, who stated that the enterprising entrepreneur was the incomparable dynamo of the process of creating wealth and that there was "circular flow," or reciprocal influences between technology and productive organization. He pointed out that creators introduce new goods, which in turn generate new means of production and administration that are immediately introduced in new markets. This economic stimulus provokes competition among economic agents determined to improve and make cheaper products. In other words, innovation unleashes feverish economic activity that continually raises the standard of living of the leading societies. In our day, this assertion is evident to anyone who has closely followed, say, the progress of information technology. From the first IBM machines the field has grown to include ever cheaper, faster, smaller yet more powerful computers, the Internet, and virtual markets that allow for wider trading of other goods. How much of the growing prosperity in the United States since the 1970s, the so-called "new economy," is due to the multiple uses of the computer?

What, ultimately, is the key to the world's most successful societies? According to Schumpeter, it is the combination of the energetic entrepreneur, Carlyle's *captain of industry*, with the innovative genius. When societies gave rise to these individuals through the right institutions — a market economy, rule of law, and reasonable rules — the societies took off. When one or more of these elements were missing, things went awry.

But Schumpeter's persuasive explanation of the dynamics of economic development leaves unanswered why some European nations experienced an explosion of scientific and technical creativity while others, such as Spain and Portugal and consequently countries in Latin America, did not. The premise of this chapter holds that, to a large extent, inclusion on the list of scientifically and technically leading countries depends on each nation's education and the worldview citizens adopt as a result.

In any history — and this presumes to be a different kind of history book — it is essential to know when the key institutions took shape, especially education. Formal education — what is learned and how and why it is learned — has a primary importance in understanding the subsequent behavior of nations. Today, few believe that there are any biological differences among the "races," or among human groups. Nevertheless, there are differences in the information they gather and in the education they receive, including the value systems they inherit.

From these values stem a worldview that generates behaviors, duties, and, naturally, results, all of which occur through a constantly changing process that allows us to conclude there is no fixed destiny. The very poor England of the thirteenth and fourteenth centuries became the great empire of the eighteenth and nineteenth. China, richer and more cultured than Europe in the fifteenth century, froze in its millennial traditions. The feared Spain of the 16th century gradually became relatively insignificant in modern times. Japan and Russia moved in the opposite direction, the latter with an ascendant trajectory from the backward, almost uncivilized principality of Moscow to the emergence of the USSR. Even given the brutality with which it occurred, this great leap is nevertheless astonishing.

THE FUNDAMENTALS OF TRADITIONAL EDUCATION

Expecting to find ancient Asian lands abundant in spices, the conquistadors disembarked instead in the New World, a frustrating turn of events. Immediately they stumbled upon the primitive societies of the Arawak Indians, in which there did not exist, or in which the Spaniards could not distinguish, signs of an organized educational system. They assumed the Indians were hardly better than savages.

Nonetheless, the Spanish lost no time in confirming their error. When they reached Mexico, and the highly complex Aztec culture, they noted (and not without admiration) that the natives had a very structured educational system, which included a correlation between social class and the teachings to which students had access. Among the poor peasants, known as the *mecehualtin*, the largest group in the social pyramid, fathers were responsible for teaching their sons the tasks of agriculture and the norms of cohabitation with others. It was socially acceptable for them to resort to severe punishments, including exposing the child's skin to the stinging smoke of burning chilies. Mothers, in turn, educated their daughters in the proper duties of their gender and tended to be less strict.

The aristocratic caste, the *pipiltin*, was given an education that would have held Plato in high regard. Young males were taught to be model gentlemen. If they would one day belong to the ruling class, they needed to learn to be valiant, generous, and sober minded, always in control of their emotions. Upon reaching puberty, they were separated into two basic groups: those who joined the *calmécac*, destined for the priesthood or the imperial bureaucracy, and those who were sent to the *telpochali* to attend a kind of military school, a basic element of a fundamentally warrior civilization. The *mexicas* of the highest social hierarchy were those who joined the *calmécac*, perhaps because they were the repositories of Aztec science and technology. They learned astronomy, civil engineering, and mathematics, as well as religious hymns and their culture's cosmogony, all under the attentive supervision of priests who controlled the lives of these youngsters with the same rigor seen in the most severe Christian monasteries and with some of the same moral suppositions. They forbade sexual relations, for instance, and used exemplary punishment to anyone caught violating the norm.

If such was Cortés' experience of the Aztecs, Pizarro and Almagro had quite another experience in the Andes. The Incas had a more rudimentary system of education, one that led the Spanish to think they made a deliberate effort to keep the masses subdued since the Incan regime was in some respects a totalitarian state. In any case, Incan science and technology did exist, as the impressive Machu Picchu ruins testify, and as the other urban constructions still preserved in Cuzco show. Nevertheless, little of pre-Colombian culture in general survived the Conquest of America. The culture soon commenced to be Hispanic, despite all the sophisticated attainments of the native peoples documented in Bernardino de Sahagun's *General History of the Things of New Spain* (1558-1569). This religious thinker compiled information about the Aztecs' astronomical and medical knowledge; and in a very curious tract co-written in Latin, two of the first Indians the Spanish licensed in medicine, Juan Badiano and Martin de la Cruz, surprised the Europeans with their *Libellus de medicinalibus Indorum herbis,* sharing a good portion of Aztec learning in botanical matters. In addition, there was Diego de

Landa's valuable book, *On the Things of the Yucatán*. Ironically, having burned innumerable Mayan texts for heresy, Landa himself contributed to our knowledge of the Mayas through his work.

The Spaniards' first educational institutions in America were created for the Indians and not the whites. This was hardly a matter of altruism, as the Spanish were motivated by both missionary zeal and the need for social control. The Incan leaders were not the only ones to use the education system to keep the people subdued. The conquistadors, almost all young men, had no plans to improve their education, but the Crown owed Rome the conversion of the natives, and this obligation quickly became an effort to accomplish their transculturation.

The Spanish language was used teaching not only to introduce the word of God and "the true religion" to the Indians, but also to strip them of their own cultural systems and turn them into semi-Spaniards. Franciscans and Dominicans, with some Mercedarians, Augustinians, and later Jesuits, landed in the Americas determined to proselytize the great indigenous masses — controlled by swords and cowed by the Spaniards' "thundering" firearms and their horses — to the Catholic faith and a basic variant of Spanish culture. It soon became clear that the large number of children was overwhelming the priest-teachers, and too few laymen had any real teaching vocation. How could they educate the Indians with such limited resources? By transforming the sons of the ruling Indians into models for the rest of their people. If the Spanish managed to educate the offspring of the Indian elite, the next generation would lose any will to resist.

It was no easy task. To the indigenous aristocratic caste, allowing the invaders to educate their sons, though it certainly was a route to material rewards, was repugnant. To avoid the ignominy, some nobles gave plebeian boys to the teachers in place of their true descendants, an exchange that brought with it certain social upward mobility. Others simply fled. Most, crushed by defeat, acquiesced, and saw their children brainwashed into becoming members of a mestizo variant of Spanish culture.

The children, naturally, learned little in the "Indian schools." Their education mostly consisted of religious history, reading and writing, basic math, hymns (they sang often, a fact that seemed to please the priests as much as the children), and some professional trades. They were not expected to be either original minded or independently creative, so their instruction was formal and repetitive. Boys were given priority, although schools for girls did exist. Also, in Mexico, schools began to be founded for a third student body, the mestizos. The Spanish hoped to turn the most talented young Indians into a Christian cadre capable of influencing the indigenous society. In some cases, when they were exceptionally intelligent and dedicated, the Indians received an education equal to that of the most cultured Spaniard. Such was the case for Latin-versed Hernando de Ribas and Antonio Valeriano, excellent linguists who mastered Spanish and Latin.

THE FIRST UNIVERSITIES AND THE SURVIVAL OF THE PAST

In the middle of the 16th century, three universities already existed in Latin America, quite an exceptional fact given the low demographic density of Spaniards in the New World. (Although Indians could enroll, very few did.) The University of Santo Domingo was founded in 1538; the universities in the viceroyalties of Mexico and Lima were begun in 1553. They were created with the University of Salamanca and to a lesser extent the University of Alcalá de Henares as models. They offered five disciplines: theology, canonical law, jurisprudence, medicine, and the arts. The rector had so much authority over professors and students and over the educational process — including judicial competitions that could sentence every punishment except mutilation and death — that they oftentimes clashed with colony bureaucrats and even the viceroys.

Just as in Europe, Latin was the language used for study. Classes were roughly an hour long, timed by sand-filled hourglasses. Unless called upon, the students normally sat in silence. To graduate, it was enough that one regularly attend class. Examinations were given not by subject but by grade level. When students completed their studies for licenses or doctorates, it was customary to submit them to cruel gags known as *vejámenes*. The classes were taught in the medieval style (which was devised in order to deal with, among other things, a shortage of books) and consisted of lectures and commentary on texts made from different literary, historical, spiritual and allegorical perspectives.

This style of teaching, the essence of medieval pedagogy, was used in some cases up to the eighteenth and 19th centuries. In general, students read the *auctores* (from which comes the word *auctoritas*, or authority). These were irrefutable creators/thinkers who had uncovered truths, which, once disclosed, were beyond debate. This was the "scholastic" method, consisting of rediscovering truths rationally by way of the meticulous review of text annotation and not by studying reality or experience. *Verba, non res* — the word, not the thing — was important. When any doubt arose about an interpretation of the texts, students resorted to the *disputatio* to resolve it. Still, disputation was not a free exercise of imagination. It was a kind of pre-established verbal dueling in which everything was mechanically argued following inflexible rules. Why this almost fetishist fascination with the word, especially the written word? For Catholic ideologues, the final goal of understanding was to delve into the Scriptures. A religion founded on the unassailable veracity of certain sacred books revealed to a chosen few had to be capable of attaining wisdom by means of the word.

In medieval times, the list of *auctores* was almost always the same: Donato for grammar, Cicero and Quintilian for rhetoric, Galen and Constantine the African for medicine, Justinian's *Corpus iurus civilis* for law, and Porphyry and Boethius for philosophy. Over time, the *auctores* might change, but the alumnus — literally "he who receives nutrition" — was force-fed with texts that had to be assimilated without question. Few things seemed more ungrateful in the eyes of God than "intellectual arrogance." It was not even enough to be a renowned teacher to put forth original ideas. One of the bitterest complaints by Roger Bacon against Albertus Magnus, later proclaimed a saint and *doctor universalis*, was that the German at the University of Paris advanced his own opinions as *autenticas*. In Bacon's eyes, Magnus' reasoning was invalidated — not because his ideas were weak or there were errors in his approach, but because they lacked *auctoritas*.

Italian essayist Eugenio Garin elegantly commented on this system in *Education in Europe: 1400-1600*: "The defining of the structures of school and the rigid establishment of its methods, books, and forms of teaching crystallized a form of thought, or a system of reality and life, in rigid schemas that, born of fluid reasoning, attempted to fix it in valid formulas forever. These formulas represented both the grandeur and limitations of what has been called precisely *scholastic*. Its grandeur consisted of having drawn up at the schools a system capable of assuming universal value; its limitation was having believed in the validity of that system, considering absolute that admirable learning 'technique' that had been defined particularly in Paris and Bologna in the domains of theology and law."

By the time the universities were founded in America, this pedagogic system was in total crisis. The rebellion against the old scholastic pedagogy was a very important aspect of the Renaissance. It was in the 15th and 16th centuries that people began speaking of *studia humanitatis*, or studies in the humanities, consisting of a reconsideration of Greek and Roman classics, only without the tunnel vision imposed by traditional scholasticism. Two important events transpired that immediately converged in western Europe: Gutenberg's printing press and the influx of erudite Byzantines fleeing the Ottomans in 1453 and bringing Hellenic manuscripts with them. It was no longer necessary to read the classics for the purpose of seeking validation of Catholic dogma. They could be read simply for the pleasure of knowing. Man became the center of creation, his existence to be celebrated and his environment scrutinized with a more rational and unprejudiced attitude. This triggered a powerful protest against the monks, to whom the grave responsibility of managing education was assigned.

In effect, the Church had taken up the reins of education the moment the Western Roman Empire fell in the fifth century. This meant that the Church preserved Roman pedagogy, the Latin system that itself had been derived from the Greek model of the *heptatucon*, based on the classic metaphor of the seven columns supporting the temple of wisdom.

These seven pillars were grammar, the study of proper communication; rhetoric, the art of persuasive argument; dialectic, the use of logic to distinguish between good and evil; arithmetic, the process of quantifying facts through numbers; music, the mastery primarily of songs but also of instruments; geometry, the measurement of the dimensions of the earth, equally important to agriculture and construction; and astronomy, the understanding of the laws that govern the motion of heavenly bodies.

The seven elements comprised the liberal arts, which were considered to make man free, removing the blinders of ignorance and the servitude that weighs down upon him in the real world (although Seneca, the Roman Stoic who was born in Córdoba, Spain, believed that they did not improve man's lot, that his improvement was only possible through education in the correct values). The first three disciplines formed the *trivium* and allowed for the individual expression of the spirit. Elegance and eloquence were the aim, and form was the focus. Thus arose the modern usage of the adjective *trivial*. The more substantive matter, by contrast, was found in the last four disciplines of the *cuadrivium*, wherein rested reason. These categories have survived until today, and exist not only in our language but also in our systems of teaching. In present-day terms, the *trivium* was arts and letters, and the *cuadrivium* provided the origin of the pure sciences, although later law and medicine were added.

The Latin educational tradition that the Church inherited was based at its most elemental level on the *pedagogus* or *litterator* who taught children to read and write on waxed tablets with a *stylus*. Children learned to count with their fingers, and indeed in the Roman numeral system the numbers are represented by symbols reminiscent of the hand and fingers, and the zero did not exist. Teachers were authorized to strike students with a type of rod, a *ferula*, and they did so with such force that the history of pedagogy — thanks to Horatio's accounts based on his own childhood experiences — has passed down the Spanish word *orbilianismo*, named after Orbilio, to describe the brutal behavior of an instructor who viciously punishes his charges.

The second level of the Latin education centered on *grammaticus*. In essence, it was a deeper form of lecture, with intensive exercises requiring the memorization of Latin and Greek texts, usually beginning with Virgil's *Aeneid* and afterward tackling Homer's *Iliad* and *Odyssey*, the verses of which students had to analyze and classify one by one. The third and last level was the responsibility of the *rhetor*, and few youths ever reached this formative phase. With the *rhetor*, students had to perfect their expressive capacity. Being a great communicator was the ultimate virtue of intellectuals, including politicians (a frequent duality among the Romans), not only because it revealed a particular skill but also because it was thought that an orator's eloquence demonstrated an elevated morality. The greater the eloquence, the finer spirituality the person was believed to possess.

The most important *rhetor* in Latin culture was, in fact, a Roman born in Spain (in *Calagurris*, today Calahorra, a town in Rioja) and educated in Rome. His name was Marcus Fabius Quintilianus (30-96 A.D.), also known as Quintilian. Educators consider him, with good reason, the founder of modern pedagogy, a rather impressive designation for a man who lived nearly two thousand years ago. Quintilian was a distant relative of Emperor Domitian, whose nephews he taught in the unequalled Latin oratory model of Cicero. In his retirement, Quintilian wrote twelve books (or scrolls) entitled *Institutiones Oratoriae*, in which he systemized for posterity the most efficient sequence for organizing discourse — invention, arrangement, style, memorization, and delivery — by adding to the structure a clear and logical simplicity: introduction, exposition, and demonstration.

Yet, it was not Quintilian's skill as a *rhetor* that inspired the admiration of educators, but rather, his pedagogic beliefs, such as his stance against corporal punishment; his teaching methods using games, competitions, and prizes; his observation that education begins at home, in the cradle, and not in the classroom; and his defense of the public school as the ideal venue for training children by imitation (today called "socialization") in lieu of the home with a tutor (who was generally a worn down Greek slave). Quintilian's book and ideas, rediscovered in 1470 thanks to the fortuitous appearance of an ancient manuscript, spurred on Renaissance humanists then trying to reform education.

The essence of a Latin education was, without a doubt, form, word, and gesture. Elegance was sought above all — the cultured quotation from some classical text, the pronunciation of a phrase in the right tone of voice and with the perfect gesture. The future was not import; such progressive thought did not exist. The notion of "science" as knowledge geared toward transforming reality had not appeared. Civilization seemed to be what Greece had achieved and Rome had perpetuated, and no one thought of changing it.

This was the Church's vision in the sixth century when it ordered that a school should be founded in France (then called Gaul) wherever a bishop lived. In 524, Pavia, Italy, witnessed the execution of the high Roman official Boethius; he was charged with treason by the German-Roman authorities. An erudite Christian whose studies had bridged Catholic theology with the Hellenic tradition of Plato, Aristotle, and Porphyry (the last a neo-Platonic philosopher), Boethius had also compiled and translated the geometry of Euclid and the astronomy of Ptolemy. His work was immensely important. *The Consolation of Philosophy*, which he wrote in jail while awaiting his execution (earning him the status of Church martyr) and its choice of authors and themes transformed Catholic culture. He designed a frame of reference, a type of proto-curriculum, and did so at a critical moment when urban centers were rapidly deteriorating, producing the rapid re-ruralization of Western Europe. Guides and canons were crucial at this time. Monasteries multiplied, providing a refuge for the learning of the age. Certain Latin values began to fade away. Penetrated by Stoicism, Christianity resisted poetry and sensuality. Frugality and even coarseness began to be appreciated.

Sixth-century Seville saw the birth of Isidore (562-633), a key medieval figure who would leave a lasting influence on education. To some degree, he amplified on the work of Boethius. Unlike the Roman martyr, however, Isidore was perfectly content with the German monarchy. Spain was then under the rule of the Visigoths, who were, at a cultural level, under the rule of the Catholic Church. The Church had kept three functions which lasted for many centuries: *docere* (teaching), *regere* (governing), and *sanctificare* (evangelizing). Isidore, who saw himself as profoundly Visigoth, was perhaps the first prominent Spaniard who did not profess Roman patriotism. In 601 he assumed the bishop's post of Seville, vacated by the death of his brother Leander. He was fundamentally an instructional bishop, and his most important duty was to oversee education. To this end, he trained priest-teachers, for whom he wrote his masterpiece *Etymologies,* an encyclopedia of 20 books focused on the roots of words. Isidore believed the essence of things could be found in the terminology used to represent them. If one could find the pure meaning of words, one was on the right path to wisdom.

Then and there, in the cult of words, medieval scholasticism took root. Isidore, later considered a saint along with his brother, became famous throughout Christendom. One could call it the School of Seville and with no exaggeration say that this was the moment of greatest "Spanish" influence on European culture. However, true to his Visigoth background, Isidore was also anti-Semitic. He drafted two texts that became widely reproduced in the Middle Ages: *Of the Catholic Faith Against the Jews* and the *Books of Differences,* written "against the perfidy of the Jews." A century later, a mild British friar — who, also canonized, was later known as Saint Bede the Venerable — became a key figure in England's intellectual formation (and possibly its first historian) after attentively studying *Etymologies.* So did his most important disciple, Alcuin, when directed by Charlemagne to organize the education and administration of the Carolingian Empire. For better or worse, classical education was saved, and the tradition would later span the ages from ancient Greece to colonial America.

In the Europe of the High Middle Ages, monks and abbots had the special responsibility of preserving culture. Monasteries proliferated and varied. In some, religious and secular families cohabited. In others — a smaller number — called in Spanish *dúplices,* clergy of both sexes lived together. For the most part, celibate males who abhorred the sins of the flesh and women who sought sanctuary from the cruel world inhabited these religious centers. To all these institutions, desperate parents offered up their children for adoption. They were known in Spanish as the *donados* (the "donated") and as *oblatos*, or *oblates*, and they were treated harshly. Isidore himself sadly recalled the punishments that his teacher Brulio inflicted on him. To escape their angry and punitive instructors, children sometimes sought refuge at the altar, where the rod of the teacher could not reach them. Some of the youths, on turning 18, chose tonsure, remaining forever within the environs of the order that adopted them. It was an exceedingly uncertain time.

The monks were to some degree like the glue holding Europe together. They established a relatively uniform cultural message. The monasteries they founded and administered were the repository of sizable libraries, often located at the highest point to allow reading in better sunlight. Each also had a *scriptorium*, in which the *librarius* (or scribe), trained from childhood and generally assisted by a proofreader, patiently attended to his work, ever threatened with severe punishment if he dared abandon his office. It was sometimes possible to purchase a good book copy from a tavern keeper, the normal intermediary between private and monastic scribes. Such a *bibliopole* was a direct ancestor of our own bookstores. When word got out about the existence of certain rare manuscripts important to the propagation of the faith, it was common to send buyers for copies to places as remote as Jerusalem. Nonetheless, it was not from the monasteries of the Middle Ages that universities evolved, but rather, from the episcopal schools founded close to urban areas in the Early Middle Ages, beginning in the twelfth and thirteenth centuries. The rural, insular monasteries served as cultural lifelines but lacked the refinement and intellectual density that eventually developed in the revitalized cities. The universities' ultimate goal was to shape Christians and thus had to be founded with papal and sometimes royal sanction. Not all Christians wished to study the same disciplines; initially, clerics and monks generally rejected the liberal arts — civil law, medicine — and took refuge in theology. In *The Catholicon*, a popular tome of the thirteenth century, Genoese Giovanni Balbi described the Church's view on lay studies. The word *laico*, or "lay," was synonymous with "idiot" and "dimwit." *Laicus* came from *lapis*, stone. In the Church's opinion, if there was anything foreign to culture, it was the quality *lapidarius*.

ARABS AND JEWS

Outside of the Catholic tradition, Arabs and Jews had a significant influence on the intellectual course of medieval Europe and by extension, on the prehistory of the Americas, an influence much greater than a contemporary reader might think. In addition to the fact that these two groups were convinced of the existence of one God and exhibited a common ancestry as direct descendants of Abraham, both Semitic peoples shared a very similar educational methodology. Arab study was based on the meticulous, thorough reading and memorization of the Koran. Jewish study took as its focus the Bible and its related texts: the Mishnah, the Talmud (both the Talmud from Babylon and the one from Jerusalem), and the Midrasin. To the Arabs, the mosque was more than a temple for prayer — it was a place where holy men taught, similar to the synagogue for rabbis.

Between the ninth and twelfth centuries, the most advanced cultures were found in the territories conquered by the Muslims and the areas inhabited by the Jews. Between the tenth and the eleventh centuries Avicenna, a Persian Muslim, reformed Arab education by separating the disciplines in a novel manner. The pure physical sciences were now chemistry, natural history, and geography; the applied sciences were medicine, astrology, mechanics, physiognomy (the analysis of character by studying the human face), oneiromancy (the study of dreams), talismans, spells, and alchemy. He divided mathematics into pure and applied — with arithmetic, geometry, astronomy, and music in the first group and calculus, algebra, mechanics, hydraulics, and the construction of musical instruments in the second. Medicine was a special knowledge in which Arabs and Jews were the great experts of the age. The Arabs were first to establish teaching hospitals, complete with gardens for cultivating medicinal plants and doctors who examined patients while surrounded by students. The medical discipline as a formal study was of Greek origin (primarily from Hippocrates and Galen). The Arabs had absorbed the Hellenic tradition and enriched it with observations and research from other cultures, such as the medical treatments of Hindu Indians Carak and Susruta. Granted, astronomy is attributed to Ptolemy and geometry to Euclid. But calculus and geometry also had more remote and intricate origins: India, Persia, and Babylon, where the zero was first introduced. The Arabs served as a "people bridge," transmitting knowledge and institutions capable of assimilating diverse influences as they undertook campaigns to expand Islam throughout Asia, Europe, and Africa.

Avicenna's role among the Arabs was similar to Maimonides' among the Jews. Also a physician, Maimonides wrote manuals on hygiene and proposed study techniques that even today hold value in the West, such as limiting the ideal class size to 25 students. A Jew born in Córdoba, he spent a great part of his life among Muslims; at one stage he moved to Alexandria, where he became a physician to the sultan Saladin. The esteem of his fellow Jews was due mainly to his commentaries on the vast Judaic tradition of the Mishnah. Other Catholic thinkers — namely, Thomas Aquinas — drew from Maimonides' reflections on the work of Aristotle and his attempts to reconcile the Greek thinker's philosophy with Jewish theology, documented in Maimonides' work, *The Guide for the Perplexed.*

Arguably, the most educated people in the Middle Ages were the Jews, particularly those who over the centuries had settled in Spain. These were the *Sephardim*, the sons of *Sepharad* (the Jews' name for Spain). In an age when illiteracy was almost the rule, among the Jews it was an exception, thanks to their devotion to sacred books. In addition to using Saturdays for meditation and reading, "all Israelites had the duty to reserve a portion of the day and evening for study." They were perhaps the only people that placed intellectuals at the top of the social scale. "A wise and studious bastard has priority over an ignorant high priest," states a well-known Jewish maxim. Ignorance was a stigma. Hence, each community maintained its teachers, and philanthropy was seen as a sign of greatness. The Jews even led their youngsters through a curious ceremony. They covered the Hebraic alphabet with honey, and the children were asked to lick the letters, a symbolic manner of expressing the nourishing nature of culture. It also provided the children with a positive memory associating the alphabet: not with the teacher's rod, but a savory and sweet taste.

The Jews were great patrons of, and contributors to, educational institutions. They produced excellent mathematicians — a discipline related to the finances where they tended to excel — and celebrated astronomers, to such an extent that the field was known as "the Jew's subject." Because they were noted astronomers and mathematicians, it was no surprise that they developed the most advanced cartography of the age and built fine navigational instruments, specifically in Majorca. This fact has caused more than one historian to ponder a Jewish connection to Columbus, perhaps via a historian named Abraham Zacuto. Another Jewish scholar of the mid-fourteenth century, Isaac Israeli, wrote *Yesod'olam, Fundamentals of the World*, truly an encyclopedia of the astronomy of the age.

The Jews' high levels of education and presence in the peninsula rendered another benefit to the Spanish. They served as a bridge between the Arab and Christian populations and between Greek and Latin culture. Apart from Hebrew and Aramaic, many of their scholars knew Latin, Greek, and Arabic, plus the peninsula's two most important languages, Castilian and Catalan. The first translation of the Bible to Castilian was not, as commonly believed, that of Casiodoro Reina in 1569, but of Moses Arragel, who translated it from Hebrew 150 years before. In 1383, King Peter IV of Aragon ordered the Jews to translate Maimonides to Catalan. They probably did so from the Arabic, the language Maimonides used — as did Majorcan scholar Raymond Lully — to write his books on medicine. At times, translations were from Castilian to Catalan and vice versa.

Small wonder that Spain suffered an enormous loss after the expulsion of the Jews. Not only was the economy weakened by the sudden absence of its best financial experts and businessmen, but the culture was also divested of the most skilled and knowledgeable segment of its intelligentsia. The Jews had already developed a rationalistic and empirical approach, derived specifically from the followers of Maimonides, and could have assimilated the scientific and technical revolution that later transpired in the 16th, 17th, and 18th centuries. Clear signs of that revolution existed in 1492, when Queen Isabella the Catholic and her husband, Ferdinand of Aragon — apparently with the enthusiastic support of Spanish society — committed the folly of banishing hundreds of thousands of their finest subjects without realizing the damage they were causing the Sephardic Jews and themselves. It was a mutilation comparable with — although on another scale, without the aim of genocide — what occurred in the 20th century when Hitler's Germans destroyed the Ashkenazi Jews, the great segment of Jews in the German and Central European traditions that had been so vital to the development of the sciences in the Old World.

But not all Jews abandoned Spain. A good portion of them chose to convert to Christianity, some long before facing the dilemma of either accepting Christ or being forcibly expelled from the country. From this group of converts, perhaps the most surprising and fascinating case was that of the great Rabbi of Burgess, Solomon Ha Levy, who was baptized at the end of the fourteenth century and took the name Pablo de Santa Maria (Paul Saint-Mary), baptizing his five children, as well (some of whom became bishops, like him). Along with the fervently anti-Semitic Vincent Ferrer, he became a theological advisor to Pedro de Luna, who became antipope under the name Benedict XIII. He also contributed to what has since been called the School of Burgess, a cultural movement with many of the elements of pre-Renaissance humanism.

The Revolution That Changed the World

The 16th century was a time of great turmoil. Religious wars devastated Europe. Nations were reconfirming their identities with the resurgence of vernacular languages (Luther translated the Bible into German as a way of breaking with Rome and the Latin-speaking clerical hierarchy), and the old scholastic university tradition was strongly rejected by eminent humanists, among them Erasmus, Juan Luis Vives, and Philip Melancthon, the great German educator and friend of Luther, just to name a few. François Rabelais, a Franciscan and later a

Benedictine who was also a physician from Montpellier (along with Padua one of the best medical universities at the time), began publishing his five books known as *Gargantua and Pantagruel*, one of the great narratives of French literature and a masterpiece of humor and runaway fantasy. What did such fierce satire conceal? Something quite evident to the readers of the age: a scathing criticism of traditional education. Unsurprisingly, the Sorbonne was first in line asking for the author's head and a ban on the books. (The books were duly banned but Rabelais was spared, thanks to the intervention of a friend who was a cardinal.)

The conflict at the Sorbonne reflected a greater problem fomenting in all of Europe. Education was becoming a battleground. For Catholicism, the school and the university were instruments of social control. The same held true for Protestantism, after Britain's King Henry VIII broke with Rome and prohibited Oxford and Cambridge from allowing Catholics to graduate. Intolerance permeated all camps. In Geneva, John Calvin, the great educator, provoked the execution of 58 people for religious heresies. Among the victims was Spanish thinker Miguel Servet, whose ideas were unorthodox, like Calvin's — but they clashed in their beliefs about the Trinity.

The profound educational reform then taking place in the Protestant sectors of Germany frightened the Catholic countries. The Germans changed their instructional methods, seeking to consolidate the regions with the idea of being one nation. A teacher named Valenti Friedlan, better known as "Trotzendorf," reproduced in the schoolroom a miniature republic complete with old Roman dignitaries — senators, queastors, and consuls — and declared himself dictator. He also established laws and had violators judged by 12 senators. Trotzendorf intended for education to prepare a child for adult life by instilling a sense of responsibility and voluntary submission to adult rules. Before long, the Protestant educational reforms began to bear fruit. There is documented proof that in the following century the literacy level in Protestant areas was higher than in Catholic regions. At the end of the 17th century, 75 percent of the French were illiterate, while only 55 percent of Germans were illiterate (these figures are indicated by the notary documents of the period and can be estimated on the basis of evidence of the number of people who could sign their names on official papers). The Reformation of Luther and Calvin, the roots of which had little to do with education, wound up having considerable success in that area.

The Catholics did not ignore these Protestant triumphs; they were worried by them. At the insistence of Charles V, Pope Julius III, with little enthusiasm, convened the Council of Trent (1545-1563). The German-Spanish emperor selected even the location, and it had to be convened three times for lack of interest. One Erasmist sector of the Church hoped that Trent could bring reconciliation with the Protestants, but the opposite occurred.

The clash was only amplified. The Counter Reformation was born, with four primary weapons for its defense. The first was the theologians who drafted the deliberations of the Council, able thinkers who organized theoretical refutations of Protestantism. Ultimately, the debate with the Protestants was theological, a dispute about the salvation of the soul. The second weapon was the Inquisition. In the thirteenth century, Emperor Frederick II had formed a tribunal to judge heretics. The Council of Trent revitalized it, turning it into a mighty arm of repression. The third was the *Index,* which the period's "thought police" used to judge and classify books. Works that were heretical, sinful, or were thought to contradict known truths were listed on the *Index.* They had to be destroyed. Mere possession of these books could lead to severe punishment. The fourth was the pope's newly created religious order, the Society of Jesus, the Jesuits, which surged with powerful impetus.

The order's founder was a Basque nobleman, Ignacio López de Recalde y Loyola, or Íñigo de Loyola, a soldier wounded near Pamplona in 1521. During his convalescence, he had a mystical experience that inspired him to create a religious order, which fit Rome like a glove. Apart from the three conventional vows — poverty, humility, and chastity — Ignacio added a fourth: unconditional submission to the pope. It was exactly what the pontiff needed at a time when half of Christendom questioned his authority. The Jesuits grew at a surprising speed. Without a doubt, much was due to their founder's personality. Ignacio was of exceptionally strong character, and he had enormous discipline as well as an apostolic enthusiasm of such magnitude that even the Inquisition was suspicious of him and at one point jailed him. Another factor, which can be attributed to a stroke of luck, was the quality of the first Jesuits, among them three exceptional former Franciscans: Francisco Javier, Francisco de Borja, and the youngest and most erudite, from a later generation, Francisco Suárez. Others from this group who also made history include Diego Laínez, a key voice at Trent, and Claudio Acquaviva.

Very quickly, Jesuit educational institutions flourished. Ironically, education had not been Loyola's original goal. His own academic formation came late in life and was somewhat deficient. Initially, he had planned to devote himself to preaching among the Turks, but his work soon changed direction. Perhaps the change was an evolution born of two works, *The Constitutions* and *The Spiritual Exercises*. From these sprang an effective pedagogy based on the strengthening of character and introspection. The Jesuits also developed educational techniques very similar to those of their Lutheran adversaries, using prizes and role-playing. They divided students into Romans and Carthaginians, for instance, and established reward systems, or what modern behavioral psychologists would call positive reinforcement. At the end of the 16th century, Jesuit pedagogy was systematized into the *Ratio studiorium*. An inclusive method used in all the disciplines; it consisted of a pre-lecture, a lecture, exercises, and repetition. The Jesuits discovered the ways memory focused knowledge in an efficient manner. All this was done with an almost military discipline. As a consequence, many students developed a sort of *esprit de corps*, a pride in having been taught by the Jesuits, who soon became the Church's most erudite order, requiring 17 years of study.

However, not everyone was happy with the Jesuits. Jealousy and ill will were aroused in the Church, as well as concern that they were amassing too much power. They became hegemonic in Spain and eventually America. In France, they controlled a significant portion of the educational system and in Poland, almost all of it. Other orders accused them of arrogance. Governments felt insecure with a group whose declared and immovable loyalty was to the pope and not the crown. All of these elements finally culminated in 1773 with the dissolution of the order and the expulsion of its members from numerous countries, including some in Latin America, especially the territories under the Bourbons. (The order would be re-established in 1814.)

In any case, the Protestants perceived them as their most formidable adversaries. Some eminent ex-students acidly criticized them, citing their authoritarian attitude and inflexible rigidity. The most famous of these detractors was no less than Rene Descartes. Anemic and lethargic, obstinately solitary, a sometime soldier and the son of a well-to-do judge, Descartes dedicated part of his very popular *Discourse on Method* (actually a prologue to three scientific essays, "*Dioptrics*," "*Meteorology*," and "*Geometry*") to disqualifying his Jesuit education at La Fleche. He believed it neither gave him a clear sense of his life nor a rational way to distinguish truth from falsehood.

The repercussions for Descartes' criticism of the Jesuits were disproportionate. The Jesuits prohibited his texts in their schools. They felt the philosopher introduced a concept that went against the very heart of scholastic Catholicism: that one did not reach truth by revelation or by explanations from authorities, but by doubting everything through the most rigorous introspection. Saint Thomas and the elaborate artifice of his work had come tumbling down with one blow. If man could reach truth by a reason unadorned with transcendental powers, then what role remained for the Church? According to Descartes, nothing for the human being was certain save the verifiable fact that he could reflect on things and ideas. Everything might be false. Everything could be a deception of the senses or even of some perverse devil, except the certainty that one was thinking — *cogito, ergo sum*.

This reasoning, as a matter of fact, had already been advanced by Saint Augustine in the fifth century. With this idea as the guiding principle, a method of four phases was then followed: accepting only what was absolutely evident, dividing difficulties into small units to adequately analyze them; verifying the knowledge needed to organize responses in an increasingly complex order, or create a synthesis; and finally, carefully enumerating the analysis, revision, and synthesis. Paradoxically, Descartes was able to develop his method from the mathematics the Jesuits had taught him so well and probably also (why not?) from the spiritual exercises he practiced in his childhood during those long silences of profound introspection.

While Descartes mined philosophy and theology for a theoretical construction later known as "methodical doubt," other scientific thinkers took a different route that led to the same conclusion. Englishman Francis Bacon, the father of empiricism, was possibly the most influential. A man of the state, rich from birth, who fell into disgrace at the end of his life, Bacon wrote several works that garnered wide attention, including *The Advancement of Learning*, *Novum Organum*, and *New Atlantis*, the last of these posthumously published and one of the period's several utopias. Bacon made an assertion that became central to modern science: that truth could only be reached by experimentation. The scientist's task was to explore physical phenomena through repeatable and verifiable experiments. Bacon proposed the creation of what he called "the House of Solomon," an immense laboratory and bank of information. While Descartes hoped to reach scientific truth using reason and to express his discoveries in mathematical language, Bacon proposed to start with a hypothesis, carry out the experiment, repeat it, and then use the results to formulate a law of nature. Why this great effort in the quest for knowledge? The answer may be the crux of Bacon's reasoning and one of the turning points of modern history: to develop techniques that would benefit humanity. Apart from experimental methodology, Bacon advanced the idea of progress as an objective of science and intellectual inquiry. Empiricism and utilitarianism had begun to overlap. The empirical method could transform reality. Utilitarianism, which took shape much later, established that good and evil were concepts relative to the contentment or discontentment they brought most people.

Bacon fixed man's vision on the future, and it was no coincidence that a century and a half later, England would be the country that led the Industrial Revolution. Bacon laid the groundwork for what followed.

Even before Bacon, something very important had taken place in Europe. On his deathbed, Polish priest Nicholas Copernicus was able to see the publication of his work, *De revolutionibus orbium celestium libri sex* (*Six Books on the Revolutions of Celestial Spheres*). In a treatise on astronomy based on mathematics, Copernicus refuted Aristotle and Ptolemy by asserting that the sun, not the earth, was the center of the universe. The earth rotated on its axis and even orbited the sun like the other planets. The book did not state, but could not avoid, a dangerous conclusion: that man's uniqueness as the center of the universe was now in doubt.

The Aristotelian-Ptolemaic astronomic architecture was useful — the earth was the center of the universe. Man had been the focus of this center, created in the image and likeness of God; Christians adored God and the pope as his vicar on earth. But if Earth was just one of several planets, why not consider humans just another species, Christianity another belief, the pope just another ordinary person? The Church took long to react, but in 1616, after the book's popularity had grown considerably, it condemned the work as a grave heresy and added it to the *Index*. Sixteen years prior, for making very similar statements (along with other heresies), Dominican Giordano Bruno had been burned in Rome. In their own way, the more orthodox Catholic theologians understood that this cosmographical revolution went against the heart of the Church and papal authority, and they tried to eradicate it.

The next milestone came from Galileo Galilei, Italian physicist, mathematician, physician, and astronomer. A musician's son, he never formally graduated and lived with much economic hardship, although he did attain teaching posts at several universities. Galileo embraced Copernicus' theories, along with the astronomical observations of the Dane Tycho Brahe and the German Johannes Kepler — it was Kepler who first discovered the ellipse-like movements of astral bodies, which was also a shocking find in light of a Catholic orthodoxy that was certain of celestial spheres and purely circular rotations. Galileo had the advantage of better telescopes, which he improved and used to observe the surface of the moon, sunspots, and Jupiter's satellites. He confirmed and enriched Copernicus' heliocentric theory over Ptolemy's with invaluable precision, using mathematics, which he felt best expressed nature. The Church, determined to defend its dogma, forced Galileo to retract his statements and cite "intellectual error." He was kept under arrest for a long time but was spared, at least, unlike Giordano Bruno. Actually, Galileo was much less bellicose than Bruno, but not servile as some have thought. Cardinal Belarmino harassed him. Another Jesuit, Lotario Sarsi, wrote a book against him. By then almost blind, Galileo wrote a rebuttal with his final work, *Dialoghi delle nuovo scienze* (or *Dialogue of the New Science*). Not long ago, at the end of the 20th century, Pope John Paul II apologized for the unjust way in which the Church had treated him and other pioneering scientists.

The university, which had been at the center of the Galileo dispute in the 16th century, began to compete with other cultural centers that were less vulnerable to bureaucratic interference and the Inquisition's persecution. The *academy* was an association of people united by the desire to know and experiment. Academies emerged in fifteenth-century Italy as a sort of complement to official teaching, and had the advantage of being spontaneous expressions of civil society. Galileo himself carried out his investigations in the Roman *Accademia del Lincei* as well as the Florentine *Accademia del Cimento*. They provided a more relaxed atmosphere than universities. Having fewer positions available, they were freer of professional competition and envy, a fact that fostered an environment of open exchange that nurtured knowledge.

The learned Cardinal Richelieu, prime minister of France, created various academies. His successor, Jean-Baptiste Colbert, a great advocate of the French state, founded the Academy of Sciences, the Astronomical Observatory, and the Botanical Garden. As an institution, however, the academy bore its greatest fruit in England. The Royal Society for Improving Natural Knowledge opened its doors in 1660, seeking, in the spirit of Francis Bacon, to benefit scientific inquiry by publishing its findings. Explicitly including the humanities among its basic pursuits, the society's projects knew no limit. Its members were bent on conquering the material world, measuring, studying, taking apart, and classifying everything. Metaphysical abstractions had no place in their exercises. This was the temple of empiricism.

In 1703 the Royal Society gained an illustrious figure as its president: Isaac Newton. Like Galileo, who he admired and considered a formative influence, Newton was a mathematician, physicist, and astronomer. He was taciturn and profoundly religious, almost mystical. He experimented with alchemy and was fascinated by optical phenomena and pure mathematics. Along with (or rather, ahead of) German mathematician Leibniz, Newton invented infinitesimal calculus. He made history by formulating the first great, truly rational and mathematical explanation of the function of the universe: the *law of universal gravitation*. Its phrasing was extraordinarily elegant yet simple: objects attract with a force directly proportional to the product of their masses and inversely proportional to the square of the distance between them. This gravitational force is responsible for the orbit of heavenly bodies.

But what was the source of this force? Here Newton the scientist became Newton the believer and attributed the source to God. With the law of universal gravitation, Newton forever banished Aristotle from scientific territory, but his acceptance of God as the beginning of all things and of continuous movement confirmed Aristotle's philosophical prestige. Was God not the engine, the first force of existence that had also imposed the universal order? Newton's universe was like a great machine with God as the operator who kept it working.

What followed was the inevitable acceleration of the collapse of the old regime. The intellectual discredit of the Catholic Church ran parallel to the de-legitimization of absolute monarchs. Ruling by the grace of God no longer seemed plausible. If science was based on reason, political power had to be, as well. It had to be based on the consent of the citizenry and on a state regulated by the rule of equitable laws. What Newton represented for science, his fellow Englishman and friend John Locke mirrored in the political world. John Locke, doctor, judge, and educator, laid the foundations for the modern liberal state.

In Locke's wake, Frenchman François-Marie Arouet, better known as Voltaire, an anti-Jesuit educated by Jesuits, added to the revolutionary discourse of the new times an effectively sarcastic tone and devilishly seductive prose. The other great precursor of modern philosophy and social science was Jean-Jacques Rousseau, of a later generation than Voltaire (although they died the same year). Rousseau's *Social Contract* was a crucial document that arose from the yearning for democratic states. He participated in the writing of the *Encyclopedia*, 38 volumes in which the project's mastermind and editor, Denis Diderot, attempted a task similar to Boethius' and Isidore's in the medieval period — only now with a scientific and rational approach. The idea was to explain all that was explainable, embrace reality, and chart it without magical or religious elements. It was the apotheosis of the Enlightenment and the definitive end of the old world order. Nonetheless, the very purpose of the *Encyclopedia* — to encompass an all-embracing vision of reality within a series of books with a certain historical perception — demonstrated the epistemological survival of the world it intended to bury. Ultimately, the *Encyclopedia* was a medieval concept. (In the last few years of the 20th century, the French attributed their country's decline precisely to "encyclopedianism.") Nevertheless, at the end of the 18th century in every European language the intelligentsia repeated the same metaphor: reason had triumphed over the darkness of the moribund medieval universe. The English called it the Enlightenment, the Germans *Aufklarung*. It was the age of light.

This whole vast movement of paradigmatic change was muted by the time it reached Spain surreptitiously, and it was barely felt in Latin America. The reasons for this are complex and not fully understood, but at least in the 16th and 17th centuries one factor was the Hapsburgs' attitude, and in particular the steely control the more orthodox clerics had over education and culture. There were eminent Spanish thinkers such as Juan Luis Vives and Miguel Servet, but they often had to emigrate to continue their work. Even as cultured and refined an individual as Friar Luis de Leon had to experience the Inquisition's dungeons.

Granted, repression was not exclusive to Spain, but evidence suggests it was worse there.

What better evidence can there be, indeed, of the climate of terror than the scientific sterility of a country that in other aspects was leading the world? It was as if scholasticism, strengthened by the Counter Reformation (essentially a Spanish movement to back the intellectual, political, and religious old guard) had been fixed in time. The important truths had already been discovered and certainties established beforehand, so further investigations were discouraged. It was dangerous to say that the earth went around the sun; a few daring university Copernicans in Spain did say it, but their voices were quickly silenced. It was also risky to teach the findings of Belgian anatomist Andreas Vesalius, who found more than 200 errors in the texts of Galen and struck Aristotle a great blow. Repeating Aristotle's obvious errors, such as saying that teeth grew constantly throughout one's life and were worn down by chewing, was safer than accepting the new anatomy. Any changes might weaken the Church's grip on society, and anything that threatened the Church was dangerous to engage in. Even though there were prominent Spaniards in all the sciences, including admirable scholars (as certified by the splendid writings of José María López Pinero on Spanish science), they launched no independent intellectual initiatives and remained subordinate to foreign scientific and technical momentum.

The brilliance of Spain in those days is visible in the dazzling paintings by Diego Velázquez and the writings of the poet whose portrait he painted, Francisco de Quevedo; in Fernando de Rojas' *La Celestina* and the anonymous, picaresque novella *El Lazarillo*, and in the works of Garcilaso de la Vega, Miguel de Cervantes, Lope de Vega, and Calderón de la Barca. This was a Golden Age, indeed, but solely in the literary and artistic arenas or, more specifically, in those pursuits that did not put one on a collision course with either the old scholastic tradition or the authorities, and did not endanger the existing order. There were wonderful writers and artists, but they lived in a culture that looked exclusively to the past and that feared and mistrusted the future. A few,

135

such as Lope de Vega, Calderón, and Quevedo (despite his political fumbling), were enthusiastic members of the establishment.

It was not that Spain lacked institutions similar to those in the rest of Europe. The Academy of Mathematics was founded in Madrid in 1582 and the Escorial, from Philip II's reign, already housed an experimental pharmacy, but they had very little weight in society as a whole. Ortega y Gasset once said that Spain never experienced the Renaissance.

It certainly never had a scientific revolution, or an Enlightenment, despite Feijoo, Jovellanos, and other "enlightened" thinkers. Spain had elements of all the trends of Europe's cultural history, but not in the quantity or quality that appeared in other places. The country never had an equivalent to Da Vinci, Galileo or Newton. Other than the stifling establishment, what can explain this deficit? Some authors have tried to suggest an explanation based on blunt, anti-scientific racism — in other words, the idea that certain races were destined by nature to be backward or sterile in the sciences. If this was the case on the Iberian Peninsula, what could one expect in the colonies? While the Old World was teeming with ideas, innovations, and iconoclastic rebellions that demolished the former order of things, across the Atlantic, syllogisms and Latin phrases were repeated tiresomely and at a much slower pace than even in Spain. True, there were about to be three centuries of *pax hispana*, but perhaps the price of that relative peace was the intellectual impoverishment of Ibero-American societies and their continued absence in the realms of technology and science. Other people, indeed, were doing the inventing. No one saw how bad this situation was or foresaw the economic and social cost to the future.

THE DEVELOPMENT OF TECHNOLOGY

How did this intellectual backwardness affect the material world of Spain and Latin America? To measure the phenomenon, we may have to begin by understanding the tightly interwoven nature of technological innovations and the many-pronged offshoots that each break-through may have. To use a well-known example, no one invented the train in a single day — it evolved from the mining industry. Exhausted miners had to excavate ore from the entrails of the earth. For this purpose, they constructed carts and placed them on wooden rails. They needed pumps to drain water. New steam machines solved the problem. Soon, carts pulled by men and mules were substituted by a primitive locomotive, greatly increasing the efficiency of coal mining. Iron foundries were built, able to reach enormously high temperatures, and iron rails replaced wooden ones. When the train came into use outside the mines, the face of nations changed. Every railway bend gave birth to an important population. If the train did not reach a town or city, the area withered. According to experts, the history of progress in the United States is also the history of the train as an urbanizing agent that "conquered" the West at a much faster pace than the wagon caravans could do.

From the improved mining technology that sparked the great capitalist economy sprang the sappers, specialists in military science. They knew how to dig, shore up, and, with the arrival of explosives, demolish. This was military engineering in embryo form. To blow up bridges or fortresses, they had to understand how to build them. War is a cruel human experience that leaves an endless legacy of inventions and advances for those who survive. Smelters that formed church bells evolved into cannon manufacturers (with the addition of gunpowder to the bell), a fact that explains why religious men, especially Jesuits, were cannon experts. The cannon is essentially a piston that moves by explosion. When the pistons are sequentially linked, it creates an internal combustion engine. Cannons were also developed smaller in size, becoming portable and ultimately taking the shape of pistols and muskets. At first, craftsmen built firearms one at a time. As with cannons and traditional swords, each weapon had its own design and name. But armies began to grow to enormous sizes, and with them grew the need to standardize weapons. To arm hundreds of thousands of men with complex weapons was a task that required mathematicians, physicians, chemists, and engineers. They made interchangeable pieces for identical weapons that shot "homologous" projectiles and were carried by uniformed soldiers marching together to the sound of drums and trumpets. The modern army that began with the Dutch in the 17th century and to which the Swiss made significant contributions was the testing ground for the Industrial Revolution still to come. The Dutch, Germans, English, French, and Italians took the lead in those processes that today we attribute to the "military-industrial complex," to use the phrase coined by President Eisenhower in the mid-20th century. The Spanish were left in the dust.

There were several reasons for Spain's stagnation, all of which have confusing exceptions. Spain was hindered by its constant xenophobia based almost always on religious grounds. While other great states encouraged the influx of artisans, Spain, a century after expelling the Jews, drove out the Moors in 1609. No fewer than 375,000 people, many of them businessmen, artisans, and farmers, left the country, while in Latin America foreigners were turned away.

Spain squandered the enormous potential for development it had enjoyed in the Middle Ages. Its monasteries had developed a strong work ethic and encouraged a productive use of time. Following the tradition begun by the Benedictines, they rang the bells seven times a day. This organization of time, as Carlos Cipolla wrote so beautifully in his essay, synchronized worker activity and greatly enhanced production and society's productivity. The invention of the mechanical clock in the thirteenth century, moreover, improved on all of it. The clock on the church steeple helped to organize people's chores. Yet, Spain was disastrously slow in developing a clock-making industry. It is unclear why. It began manufacturing them too late, and its clocks never had the prestige or quality of foreign ones — a detrimental situation and an omen, as well. Clockmakers were a combination of locksmith and goldsmith. The most meticulous artisans, they created a delicate apparatus of cogged wheels and metal bands, to which they added springs and tiny screws. Only the most skillful made them. The clock was a seminal device. Several of its mechanical principles were later used for other inventions such as weapons, mills, and motors.

The clock uniformly transmitted the movement of a needle over a sphere. Its energy was mechanical. Its "spring" tightened a metal piece that then loosened up rhythmically. Industrial development depended on creating such means of freeing energy in a systematic manner. The mill is another example. Wind or water moved its blades, which transmitted the energy to stones that grind grain or seeds. The Dutch, who had to wrest land from the sea, learned to use the mills to drain water and construct canals in their "lowland" nation. Nature's challenges made them industrious and turned them into great engineers.

The English rediscovered a principle that the Greeks had suggested centuries before the birth of Christ: steam channeled in a specific direction became a powerful driving force. They apparently first applied this finding to a toy. The steam engine multiplied the use of energy exponentially. Whereas air or river movements were unequal and unpredictable, the energy of a steam engine was stable and controllable.

The English were also the first to realize that encouraging inventors benefited all of society. As early as the 17th century, the British Parliament voted for the first law of patents. Up until that point, the Crown awarded monopolies to whomever it chose as a privilege. Now, inventors could aspire to owning their creations exclusively, usually for a long period of time. Material success had been added to the glory of invention.

The British government also offered prizes to those who solved certain technical problems or manufactured machines that met certain needs. This practice spread through Europe, with its greatest incidence in the five usual countries: England, Holland, Germany, Italy, and France, with increasing frequency in Scandinavia, as well. An interesting example involves Napoleon. Preparing for his long, indeed endless campaigns, the general needed to provide for his massive troops. "Armies," he said, "advance on their stomachs." Somehow he had to feed 800,000 soldiers in the field, so he proposed a generous prize to anyone who could find a way to preserve military rations. From this resulted vacuum packing. It later became a huge industry, in which France still maintains a respectable presence.

Steam dramatically increased the production capacity in textile manufacturing and lowered the cost of fabric; that, in turn, increased the demand for cotton and caused a surge in demand for mechanical harvesters to multiply agricultural production. As with clocks and cannons, however, Spain — not to speak of its American colonies — barely participated in these developments.

Other objects, humbler but nonetheless tremendously important for progress, also got little or no attention in Spain. Spectacles, like clocks, had been around since the thirteenth century, but their use was less common in Spain than in the rest of Western Europe. Intellectuals and creators began losing their sight at 40, the typical age for the onset of farsightedness. Glasses could have helped them, especially after the arrival of printing in Europe made deficient sight even more odious. Velázquez painted Quevedo wearing spectacles (since then called *quevedos*), but this was an unusual image.

Lenses, and glass in general, were advancements that greatly modified industrial processes. Large windows made it possible to extend the factory work day, and eyeglasses prolonged workers' ability to work. As Lewis Mumford intelligently observed, lenses allowed a cleaner and neater existence by making it easier to spot dirt and disorder. Indeed, Flemish paintings captured the spotless homes of the bourgeois Belgians and Dutch. Lenses were also turned skyward in telescopes and downward in microscopes to delve into matter. The consequence was the almost instant discovery of a hidden world of abominable, diminutive creatures, previously unsuspected enemies. In the same way that technical discoveries were interrelated, scientific observations also intertwined in an almost natural manner.

After steam came electricity (like so many things, presaged by the Greeks), and production once again made a quantum leap. Hard machines made of molten steel, cast at high heat — with gears in which one could detect traces of the clock or the cannon or the loom — since every invention carries in its mechanical memory the hybrid history of ever interconnected technologies, began spewing forth by the hundreds of thousands objects previously produced piecemeal. The Industrial Age accelerated.

It is sufficient to view a 17th century house, when Aeolian energy still reigned and production was mostly manual. View it in the 18th century, during the heyday of steam, and return to it in the nineteenth, the age of electricity. What do we see with the passing of time? More *things*. A motley assortment of objects. The world had become more colorful thanks to a greater number of things to be had at progressively cheaper prices. The average man — who once could only buy wheat, some meat, and a few yards of coarse cloth — began purchasing hundreds of industrial goods and enjoyed an elevated standard of living. Seventeenth-century wills passed down gloves, used capes, doublets, and tablecloths; the 19th century brought a wider variety of goods.

In a way, progress is precisely that — possessing more objects, accelerating movement, reducing manual labor and making life more secure and comfortable. Progress, moreover, rests in the universities, academies, and laboratories, all united by science, technology, business, and trade and regulated by the proper legal institutions. Another consequence of the accumulation of objects was the refinement of the other senses. Where glasses had improved vision, the reduced cost of perfumes contributed to a more demanding sense of smell and of fabrics to a heightened sensitivity to tactile pleasures. Silk and velvet descended the social scale, passing from princesses to plebeians. Sensual pleasure had been made democratic.

Spain, Latin America, and Portugal had lost the historical opportunity of post-Renaissance modernization. Though they did enjoy the positive changes it brought, they did so passively, always as the receptors of technical and scientific innovations born outside their borders. Hence Latin America's deficient development, the anemia of its industry, and the marginal creativity of its educational institutions.

Poor social habits also resulted, such as scoffing at someone who dared to think originally, surrendering to a passive life, and reproducing lifestyles designed on other continents. Certainly it is no mistake to follow a model of civilization set by others who are successful. (This has marked Western history since before the Greeks. We are much indebted to the cultures of ancient Mesopotamia and Egypt.) It is not just the results that should be imitated, but also the innovation and creativity that went into them. To again paraphrase Schumpeter, the economist mentioned at the beginning of this chapter, one of the basic keys to prosperity is novel technical and scientific development, that thing or that service lately developed that is placed on the market to benefit consumers. Forsaking initiative in these fields and leaving it to others to invent was a sure way to guarantee Latin America's relative backwardness, which has endured until today.

7. Caudillos, Montoneros, Guerillas, And Liberals And Conservatives

In 1792 Charles IV's most notable minister, Floridablanca, terrified by news of the French Revolution, made an impressive prophecy: "We are living next to an inferno that could burn everything, destroy religion and the sovereignty of the king as well as the very existence of the monarchy itself and the classes that compose it." He was right. Soon afterward, on January 21, 1793, Louis XVI and his wife, Marie Antoinette, were guillotined despite the maneuvers and threats of the other monarchs of Europe.

Shortly before these events, Spain allied with England — until very recently its rival — and other imperial powers to encircle revolutionary France. This is not the place to tell that story, but the episode ended with the defeat of the Spanish troops, who had only one initial moment of glory. The French manipulated the Spanish monarchy's alliances to its own benefits, turning the kingdom of Spain into a virtual satellite of the Napoleonic Empire, and occupied nearly all the peninsula.

After a series of shameful betrayals and reversals in the spring of 1808, in Bayonne, France, Charles IV of Spain (who had previously abdicated and left the throne to his son Ferdinand VII — and then had reneged on his decision) accompanied by his wife María Luisa and her court favorite Manuel Godoy (the former government *factotum*), had a fierce dispute with Ferdinand and abdicated once again, only this time leaving the throne to Napoleon. The French emperor named his own brother Joseph monarch of Spain.

For his part, Napoleon, unable to contain his disdain for the Spanish royal family, drafted a *magna carta* with several progressive provisions. The Constitution of Bayonne, which inspired a later version promulgated in Cádiz in 1812 by Spanish and Hispano-American liberals, included two guarantees: money for Charles IV, Ferdinand VII, and even Godoy; with palaces and aristocratic honors included, and Spain's continuation as a Catholic kingdom.

This was the spark that ignited the war against the French in Spain and the war against Spain in America. The Spanish refused to accept the monarch's abdication and his wrenching from Ferdinand his right to the succession (Ferdinand was not as discredited as his father); in the same way, Latin Americans asked who had the right to rule over the New World. First the uprising was against the French to the cry of "Viva Ferdinand VII!" That slogan quickly became "Long live independence!" Mexico radicalized that, to: "Death to the Gachupines!" (*Gachupines* was a derogatory name for the Spanish.) In Europe, Spanish luminaries divided into pro-French and purist camps. In the Americas, almost everyone was pro-French. They admired the revolution that had ended Louis XVI's reign, and they admired the process that a few years earlier had liberated the North Americans from British control.

THE AMERICAN AND FRENCH REVOLUTIONS

In the latter half of the 18th century, the most cultured Latin Americans, just like the liberal Spanish they so closely resembled, fed on the reformist ideas advanced by the French Encyclopedists. Without being aware of each other, Colombian Anton Nariño, Ecuadoran Eugenio Espejo, Cuban Francisco Arango y Parreño, Venezuelan Andrés Bello, and Peruvian Juan Pablo Viscardo (among many others) were working in the same vein as Spaniards such as Gaspar Melchor de Jovellanos, Juan Meléndez Valdés, and economist Francisco Cabarrús. Proponents of opening up the country to free commerce and liberal reform created the

Economic Societies of the Friends of the Nation, the organizational traces of which went back to the Basques. The elite read Locke, Montesquieu, Voltaire, Rousseau, and the Encyclopedists. After the French Revolution, they discussed the *Declaration of the Rights of Man and of the Citizen*, and even reproduced revolutionary texts, a crime in the Latin American colonies (for which Nariño and Espejo spent long, cruel years in jail).

Latin Americans viewed the United States' War of Independence of 1776 with great interest. Far from suppressing the rebellion, the Spanish authorities, then enemies of England, assisted General Washington. At one point, the assistance consisted of a great military deployment — double that lent by the French — that helped take Mobile in Alabama and Pensacola in north Florida. Money was also donated. The government and colonial society of Havana raised funds to pay the revolutionary army, then on the verge of mutiny before the 1781 Battle of Yorktown. The 1,200,000 pounds of donated gold and silver, collected in six hours, bent the floor of the U.S. Army treasury.

One of the soldiers Spain sent to aid the Americans was the Venezuelan Creole Francisco de Miranda. He was possibly the most interesting political figure of this entire period, perhaps of all modern Latin American history. The son of a Spanish businessman, Miranda was born in Caracas in 1750. At 21, he moved to Madrid to join the military. He participated in the Moroccan campaign between 1774 and 1775 as a ranking captain, though his formative battlefield experience was hardly inspiring. (Another figure of the period, pre-Romantic writer José Cadalso, penned bitter writings on the mediocrity of the Spanish military life he came to know so well.)

Thus, in 1780, Miranda was on American soil in a Spanish regiment battling the English. His exposure to what the United States was then becoming awoke in him a deep Anglophilia, inspired by the contrast between the rich, orderly, and clean life of North American colonials and the life he knew in Spain and Latin America. The political enemy may have been England, but the Venezuelan admired British civic culture. He left the Spanish military and attained the rank of general in the French Revolutionary army. His the only Hispanic name listed on the Arc de

Triomphe (a fact that did not stop his comrades in arms from almost executing him). Miranda learned to gauge the difference between the two historical processes. He wrote, "Two grand examples we have before our eyes: the American Revolution and the French. Let us discreetly imitate the first and carefully avoid the fatal results of the second." It was a futile warning and Latin Americans mostly ignored it.

How did the two processes differ? The American Revolution had been carried out to guarantee the rights of individuals before the state — precisely what the Constitution, drafted by Madison in 1787, so eloquently represented. Nominally, the uprising against the English came to a head because London had imposed unjust tariffs without consulting those to be taxed. It was a revolution in the name of law against a monarchy that had violated its own rules. A republic would replace the English Crown, but the president and government institutions would not be granted the same powers as the defeated regime — all would be subject to the rule of law. The United States adopted the social contract theory of power. Power ascended from the sovereign people to their representatives, whom they converted into paid community employees subject to their approval. The representatives' authority remained clearly limited by a legal code that treated everyone as equal. The concept of government official as public servant took hold. Neither the majority nor the government could oppress individuals. The Declaration of Independence of 1776 set down the right to the pursuit of happiness, but such a right was a personal matter determined by individual needs. The state could not seek to define or impose a citizen's happiness. It could only create the means by which each individual attained success depending on his or her talent, tenacity, and luck. American democracy was not conceived, in short, as a guideline for what a citizen should do at every moment, but rather as a method to reach the decisions permitted by law. Thomas Jefferson expressed this idea when he said that he preferred to have a free press even if society could not elect the government, rather than the opposite. Individual rights were key and the state was built to protect them. This was the equality to which they aspired — not that everyone should live the same way, but that all (or all whites, rather, since slavery continued) should have the same rights. It was called *constitutionalism* and acquired in Spanish the term *estado de derecho,* as a liberal translation of "rule of law." It formed part of the English tradition that could be read in the texts of John Locke, John Milton, and utopian literature such as James Harrington's 1656 work, *The Commonwealth of Oceana.*

With this legalistic and conservative revolutionary "model," the French embarked on another type of historical process inspired by the self-contradicting philosopher Jean Jacques Rousseau. He believed that the majority had the right to impose its will, with no limitation other than that which it placed on itself, and that natural law did not exist. All law was positive, dictated by man and therefore changeable. In this aspect, the French revolutionaries, especially the radical Jacobins, were followers of Rousseau. To them, the important thing was not individual rights — despite the celebrated Declaration of Independence — but political engineering by leaders inspired by their love for humanity to impose happiness on earth. This happiness would be manifest in equality for all — not equality under the law, but equality in results. Differences in standard of living were deemed suspicious and censurable. Thus, the word "citizen" became a rhetorical formula intended to equalize all people and erase hierarchies based on ancestry. But how could they eliminate lifestyle differences and deliver the same standard of living to the common man? It was, apparently, enough for the people to concede power to the leaders of the rebellion, whose actions would be motivated by their noble impulses, with no more regulation than whatever revolutionary passion and ethics dictated. From this thinking, figures such as Robespierre, Danton, Marat, and Saint-Just rose to prominence, although later they would devour one another. This also explains the circular sequence of happenings: the blind absolutism of a Crown that could not cede power gave birth to the revolution; the Revolution's attempt to re-design the French nation gave birth to the Terror; and the Terror led to the rise of Napoleon Bonaparte, who represented another form of monarchic absolutism, except this time with the military at its power center. Like a mad dog, history chased its own tail until it bit it off.

CONSTITUTIONS AND FAILURES

For better or worse, the avatars of Latin American wars of independence have been counted a thousand times. In a childish way, some have even resorted to measuring the site where San Martín crossed the Andes to prove that Bolívar's route was more difficult and therefore more heroic than Napoleon's. It is with the memory of these wars, and the graves of their heroes, that Latin Americans constructed the political mythologies on which they based their distinct nationalities.

In reality, what took place was part of a seemingly unstoppable phenomenon that had been occurring in the West since the 17th century. First, with England's Glorious Revolution (1688-1689), absolute monarchy passed to a constitutional monarchy in which royal authority became more symbolic than real. For the most part, it was a matter of trying to impose limits on the right of monarchs and eliminating the superstition of rulers chosen "by the grace of God." The alternative required popular consent but had much more profound implications. If sovereignty resided with the people and was not inherent in the figure of the king, then it was essential to outline its space and its administrators. In other words, the end of absolute monarchy and the rise of "the people" led inevitably to the fortification of the idea of the nation-state. Being "a people" meant being from somewhere, and nationalism surged with enormous force.

The other source of authority was the Catholic Church, and the Church and religious faith in general began to wither in the new climate. The revered cult of Reason and Science was based on the humanism of the Renaissance; it progressively weakened the Church's ability to impose its hierarchies, points of view, and behavioral norms on society. At the same time, the triumph and reinforcement of Protestant reform throughout nearly all of northern Europe vastly curtailed Rome's capacity to influence political events. In Spain, for instance, it was not even necessary to await the liberals' victory to deprive the Church of many of its goods. Charles IV himself, overwhelmed by debt from his latest conflict with the French, oversaw the seizure of numerous ecclesiastical properties. At the start of the 19th century, the Church no longer generated much fear among opposing parties.

With these antecedents, inspired more by the French Revolution than by the American, with a good dose of Masonic collaboration and England's ongoing support, the colonies' insurrection against Spain finally ignited over the length and breadth of the Latin American continent. Thus rose to prominence leaders such as the Venezuelans Simón Bolívar, Antonio José de Sucre, and José Antonio Páez; the Argentines José de San Martín and Bernardino Rivadavia; Mexicans Miguel Hidalgo Costilla and José María Morelos; Colombian Francisco de Paula Santander; and Chilean Bernardo O'Higgins. Slowly, in a long conflict characterized by ups and downs that began in 1808 and ended in 1824 with the victories by Bolivarian troops in Junín and Ayacucho, Latin American continental independence was clinched, although independence did not come to the Antilles until much later. It was a happy outcome for Americans when colony-bound Spanish troops rebelled on the peninsula after the uprising of 1820, refusing to go; this gave birth to the *trienio liberal* (liberal three-year period). In any case, not until 1902 did Cuba become an independent republic after the war against Spain organized by José Martí, who died in combat. Not until 1952, moreover, did the Puerto Ricans create the Associated Free State as a formula for exercising or ceding sovereignty in a pact with the United States that recalled the British Commonwealth. As for Panama, it separated from Colombia and established an independent republic in 1903.

When Latin Americans approached the prospect of independence, they were trapped between two influences — whose differences few seem to understand — that included the Hispanic tradition and the values it sowed in the social mindset of the New World. Latin Americans' first instinct led them to propose local monarchies suspiciously similar to the ones they had just toppled. Argentine José de San Martín, the son of Spaniards and a decorated Spanish army officer in his youth, proposed just such a thing in Argentina. In Mexico, Agustín de Iturbide, another product of the Spanish military, attempted the same for a brief period before finally declaring himself emperor.

Even Bolívar, the most resolute of republicans and the most anti-Spanish among them (one of his most famous statements was, "Spaniards and Canarians, count on death even if you are indifferent"), personally legislated and drafted the Constitution of 1825 to regulate the life of the country named after him, Bolivia. He conceived the executive as a lifetime presidency with a hereditary vice presidency, aided by an aristocratic Senate composed of people specially educated to that end. Was anything more similar to a monarchy than this freak concept of Platonic political engineering destined for failure? Bolívar was seeking a variation of absolutism devoid of popular will. "Elections are the great scourge of republics," he wrote. Bolívar felt they fostered disorder, and that only the strong arm of a rigid and honorable man could stave off misfortune. The French liberal whose mind Bolívar prized above all others, Benjamin Constant, was very hard on the Venezuelan. Whoever did not place freedom above all other concerns, he countered, could not call himself a true liberal. Bolívar wished to be so, but could not bring himself to it. "They won't believe me," he wrote with melancholy about his liberalism.

How does one explain these contradictions and ambivalences common to the whole independence generation? The most obvious reason lies in a clear discrepancy between the revolutionaries' theoretical constructs and their values and the values of the societies whose public life they wanted to reorganize. The Creoles, who basically directed the insurrection on the Latin American continent — Indians and mestizos fought with equal ferocity in both camps — were quick to single out and criticize the defects of the Spanish colonial regime. It was much harder for them to admit that they shared a common worldview and sensibility with the Spaniards. The republic and the exercise of democracy demanded a sense of responsibility, experience in the administration of government property and solid personal ethics. This moral base strengthened institutions and not the reverse. It was not, however, simply a matter of promoting perfect constitutions. England did not even have a written constitution. Collective virtues and prevailing values impelled or impeded the establishment of democracy. This is why one of the last things a desperate Miranda said as he was being taken prisoner to Spain was "Schemers! Schemers! Schemers!" Bolívar, even more embittered, also said that the only sensible thing for a Latin American to do was emigrate. His fight had been in vain. He knew it and conceded as much shortly before his sad death in a corner of the Colombian coast in Santa Marta, at the home of a friend who was Spanish, but not indifferent.

GUERILLAS AND DICTATORS

It is no wonder why a revolution precipitated by an unforeseen act — the Napoleonic invasion's overthrow of the Spanish monarchy — ultimately fell into chaos and anarchy. The independents lacked clear political goals. They could not count on a well-organized leadership capable of defining means and objectives for the short, medium, and long term. They possessed no precise idea of the configuration of the state they sought to build or the government bodies they hoped to administer. They had minimal experience in self-government. Small wonder that the result of their improvisations were fierce dictatorships under which the military became the nation's backbone and at the same time its source of tyrants and continual strife. "When you don't know whey you're going," says an old adage, "you always end up in the wrong place." Latin Americans in the first half of the 19th century, save for a few exceptions, did not know where they were going. Nor did they have any clear ideas about the nation-states they felt duty-bound to build, sometimes too artificially. This is what resulted in the five Central American republics, and in Bolivia, Paraguay, and Uruguay — which were fragments of larger polities with which they shared a long history — and even in Colombia, Venezuela, and Ecuador, nations Bolívar tried in vain to sustain under the same authority that united them in colonial times.

Two strongly interrelated tensions shook Latin Americans with great severity in the newly established republics. One was the definition of local powers. They had to decide between federalism in the form of the

United States, a supposed defender of native rural values, and the more cosmopolitan centralism farther from the rural essence of the nation. Was it a fundamental question of principles, or did the two formulas cloak rivalries of another kind? Both explanations are probably true, but supposedly federalist dictatorships such as Santa Anna's in Mexico and Rosas' in Argentina frequently wound up being fiercely centralist, despite Rosas' cry, "Death to the savage centralists!"

The second issue that divided Latin American societies was of a far more obvious ideological nature. With the decades-long outrages committed by dictators and the *montoneras* (fierce rural guerillas), who substantially undermined the continent's standard of living, or after the confrontations embodied in adversarial cities and regions (Granada and León in Nicaragua, Barranquilla and Bogotá in Colombia, Guayaquil and Quito in Ecuador, Buenos Aires and the provinces in Argentina), the boundaries of conflicted ground between liberals and conservatives were very similar to the battle lines drawn in Europe. This development explains how the liberal Italian adventurer, Guiseppe Garibaldi, could so naturally join the war against the Argentine, Rosas. It was viewed at the time as just another episode of the same ideological family and the same planetary revolution that in 1848 had simultaneously exploded in Paris, Budapest, and Switzerland. It was the confrontation between an old world order — ready to fight to the death — and a new understanding of power relationships.

In Latin America, as a rule, the liberals defended secular states focused on technical and scientific progress (two key words in this group's political vocabulary) based on industrialization and urban supremacy, while the conservatives remained attached to traditional values associated to a Spanish colonial mindset, to religiousness, and to agrarian land ownership. Liberals were influenced on the whole by the small urban bourgeoisie made up of merchants, agricultural exporters, and lawyers, while conservatives leaned toward the oligarchy made up of owners of large estates. Naturally, though the religious theme was almost always present, the line separating them was not always clear and many leaders switched camps with astonishing ease. Nevertheless, the liberal-conservative fissure was sufficient enough to inflame passions, establish sides, and define enemies for a very long time. Even today, as anyone can testify who has visited Colombia, Uruguay, Honduras, and Nicaragua, the obstinate dichotomy persists, and the political parties of that ilk — among the oldest in the world — retain considerable vitality. For liberals like Sarmiento, the choice was tragically simple: civilization or barbarism. Civilization meant all that distanced Latin Americans from the Spanish and even Latin tradition and approached the Anglo-Saxon model. Juan Batista Alberdi had championed this model in *Bases and Starting Points for the Political Organization of the Argentine Republic*, which inspired the Constitution of 1853, put into practice after the overthrow of Rosas.

Latin American liberalism, despite showing in all the constitutional texts it inspired and the words of its followers that it favored civil liberties, rule of law, and respect for democratic norms that supposedly included a scrupulous separation of powers, on diverse occasions took on dictatorial forms, which it tried to validate using the excuse of order and progress. Such was the case of Porfirio Díaz in Mexico, Antonio Guzmán Blanco in Venezuela, and Rafael Núñez in Colombia. Their role models were German unifier and modernizer Chancellor Otto-Leopold Bismarck, philosopher Auguste Comte and his *Positive Catechism*, and sociologist Herbert Spencer. Núñez and Guzmán Blanco were notably cultured politicians, but not Díaz. Unlike the crude, brutal *caudillos* of mid-century emerging from the independence wars, those who arose at century's end were, for the most part, learned.

Save for the southern cone (with the exception of Paraguay), the Latin American socioeconomic landscape looked desolate at the end of the 19th century. The wars of independence — which had caused various names to be uttered in reverence — or fear (such as Páez, the name of the Venezuelan *llanero*), did not bring stable democratic republics where the poor could find prosperity. Instead, the armies formed in the struggle against Spain remained as the principal source of authority and the backbone of the different nations born during the struggles. At the start of the 19th century, the per capita income of the United States was double that of Latin America. At the century's end, the number had multiplied by seven. Why should it seem strange, then, that the frustrations of the majority were directed in large measure against the state? A century of guerillas and *caudillos*, of civil wars and sharp power shifts between suspiciously similar liberals and conservatives had deprived Latin America of a significant place in the Western world.

What is the explanation for the region's relative failure? How did the United States go from the establishment of its independence to the defeat of Spain in the war of 1898 — seizing Cuba, Puerto Rico, and the Philippines — to become the foremost power on the planet, while Latin America — excluding Argentina after the overthrow of Rosas — remained unable to shrug off tyranny and disorder? Until that moment two explanations had sufficed, both tinged by ethnic analysis: the anti-Spanish explanation blamed its colonial roots for failure, while the anti-Indian explanation attributed it to indigenous resistance to progress.

The publication in 1900 of Uruguayan José Enrique Rodó's *Ariel* — an immediate, continent-wide literary success, possibly the first — brought a different explanation. The New World had erred in forgetting the great values of Latin culture and its traditional devotion to spiritual matters, which contained a greater dignity than Anglo-Saxon materialism. It was necessary to return to the womb and exonerate Spain for Latin America's errors. Rodó was subtly anti-American, not blaming the *gringos* for Latin America's failures yet signaling the moral superiority of Latin culture. After him would come others who would reason more along the lines of political and economic analysis. Argentine Manuel Ugarte, a great polemist and pamphletist, became the major voice of "anti-imperialism." His compatriot José Ingenieros repeated his arguments, bolstered by Marxist thought following the 1917 Bolshevik Revolution. It was the birth of a stupendous alibi to explain the ills afflicting Latin Americans: poverty was the result of foreign exploitation. This simple reasoning, adorned with a thousand adjectives and conveyed by many other lateral theories — dependency, structuralism, and the edicts of liberation theologians — remained in vogue for 80 years, precisely until the so-called "lost decade," 1980-1990, when at last the undeniable examples of other underdeveloped countries such as Singapore, South Korea, Taiwan, and even Spain had leapt into the First World with the help of the "imperialist" powers, thus exposing the argument as essentially absurd.

Despite the fact that it was a dubious and apparently groundless hypothesis, anti-imperialism — expressed mainly as anti-Yankeeism in Latin America — became one of the primary means of rousing political violence on the continent, especially with the Castroite influence on the guerilla movements that plagued Central America for at least three decades from 1960 to 1990 and still threaten the very survival of Colombia as an organized nation. Within the revolutionary rationale influenced by Leninist thought, insurrectionists — Che Guevara being the best example — took as a given that local businesses and the small bourgeoisie were the natural allies of imperialism and its domestic "servants." Destroying them was therefore a valid objective, and in doing so it was essential to sever the economic ties with the West that had supposedly been wrought to guarantee the dependence of Third World nations on capitalism and thus condemn them to backwardness.

The allies of Latin American revolutionaries could, of course, be found in the socialist camp. This was, in short, the thesis put forth by Fidel Castro in the *Non-Allied Movement*. He stressed the need to partner with Moscow and its satellites since communist nations did not aspire to economic domination. With the emergence of *perestroika* and the disappearance of the whole Eastern Bloc, however, that argument collapsed from its own weight.

YANKEES AND ANTI-YANKEEISM

Were the anti-imperialist, and in particular the anti-Yankee, arguments well founded? In 1823, the United States had proclaimed the Monroe Doctrine — to the applause of Latin Americans. It sought to block the famous *One Hundred Thousand Sons of San Luis* and the Holy Alliance — which put an end to Spain's three-year liberal period and restored King Ferdinand VII's absolutism — from sailing for America to restore its empire across the sea. The U.S. had very good reasons to fear that event. In just a few years, the small perimeter of thirteen colonies had multiplied with Napoleon's "donation" of Louisiana — an act meant to punish the English — and with Spain's forced sale of Florida in 1819. The Monroe Doctrine presented what today's media would describe as a "progressive" posture, although it was not inspired by geographical solidarity but by concern that England, in the wake of the imperial fever gripping Europe, would attempt something similar in the United States. In 1812, London had not only unleashed anew the war against its former colony but also managed to humiliate it by setting fire to the U.S. capital with nearly total impunity.

A generation later, in the mid-19th century and in the midst of an exultant nationalistic wave, the U.S. took the northern half of Mexico for itself. It did so partly by forced purchases (New Mexico and California), and partly by wars of secession waged by the Euro-American colonists — many of them newly arrived Old World immigrants — wishing to separate from Mexico and join the United States, which offered the optimistic prospect of a future that would not repeat Europe's mistakes. Such was the history of the fleeting Republic of Texas, an ill-conceived step on the road to the Union. Under U.S. president of the time, James Polk, a journalist coined a term that reflected the will of the arrogant, successful Yankee society: Manifest Destiny. This supposed that God willed that, from pole to pole and coast to coast, America should be under the dominion of the United States, a nation whose virtues destined it to lead less fortunate peoples. Curiously, Karl Marx and other radicals of the period applauded this imperialist motive, convinced that the proletariat cause would advance more quickly in the economic dynamism of the United States than in the disorganized and sleepy Mexican society. This was not the only time Marx wounded the Latin American sensibility. Few of his criticisms were as offensive as those he launched against Bolívar, whom he viewed as a pathetic Napoleon imitator.

A new imperialistic era in Latin America followed the Spanish-American War of 1898 and lasted until Franklin D. Roosevelt's election in

1932. During this first third of the 20th century, when its expansionist appetite was satiated by control of Puerto Rico, naval bases in Cuba, and ownership of the Canal territory in Panama, Washington adopted a police role. It was gunboat diplomacy, and the subsequent Republican and Democratic U.S. governments were determined to maintain law and order in the Caribbean vicinity. Faced with potentially chaotic situations and the fear that other powers would send their fleets to collect pending debts, Washington intervened in Cuba, the Dominican Republic, Haiti, and Nicaragua. Usually, other than disarming adversaries (sometimes by force), it improved education and sanitation systems, organized customs houses, and trained the local military into a constabulary force, a kind of military police for maintaining order.

When Pancho Villa crossed the Texas border, the U.S. launched punitive (and fruitless) operations into Mexico, and established a de facto protectorate over the entire zone that was ultimately counterproductive. Washington attempted to forge stable democracies friendly to the U.S. and its investors. Too often this action engendered detestable dictators like Nicaraguan Anastasio Somoza and Dominican Rafael Leónidas Trujillo. When Roosevelt became president, the U.S. decided to end its futile strategy and inaugurate the Good Neighbor Policy. "We are good and they are the neighbors," incredulous Mexicans quipped. More cynical analysts described the change in strategy as "benign neglect." In any case, one of the Roosevelt government's first actions was to enact the Platt Amendment that virtually made Cuba a U.S. protectorate.

Washington's policy of non-interference in Latin American affairs lasted a very short time. First, World War II sparked tensions with governments sympathetic to the Nazi-fascist Axis, such as Juan Perón's administration in Argentina and Arnulfo Arias's in Panama, both of which the U.S. toppled with alacrity. Then the long Cold War provoked another wave of pressures and covert interventions intended to protect U.S. political and economic concerns, actions that made way for the appearance of anti-communism as a cover for the same dictators of old. Cuba's Batista, Venezuela's Pérez Jíménez, Peru's Odría, and Colombia's

Rojas Pinilla were military tyrants strengthened by anti-communism. In Guatemala in 1954, the U.S. Central Intelligence Agency (CIA) — then taking its first steps — with the complicity of some members of the Guatemalan military overthrew Jacobo Arbenz, a freely-elected colonel with leftist inclinations who had bought Czech weapons and adversely affected United Fruit Company interests. Five years later, in 1959, Fidel Castro defeated Batista's army with little resistance. He seized power, determined to lead a communist revolution and install a one-party regime a few short miles from the United States. By Cold War logic, confrontation was inevitable.

THE STATE IS OUR SALVATION

Besides anti-Americanism and anti-imperialism, another hypothesis about Latin Americans' development came to light in the early 20th century, this one promulgated by the Mexicans. The 1910 revolution that toppled Porfirio Díaz had a trace of peasant vindication — the redistribution of fertile lands — that completely changed the source of political legitimacy. Political power could only be justified if wealth was redistributed and divided equally and if it championed social justice. The state existed to redeem the poor, an idea evident in the Constitution of Queretaro of 1917. It could do so by awarding them the goods that until then had been kept in the hands of the rich.

The ideology of the "state of justice," this interventionist state, advanced quickly and naturally in a coherent direction that over the long run proved terribly onerous. To ensure Latin America's prosperity and progress, this ideology posited, it was necessary to turn the state into the great engine of the economy. The theory was simple — local capital was scarce and the capacity to absorb technology minimal. In this view, private enterprise pursued selfish ends not always convenient for the welfare of society. Only a powerful, impartial entity like the state, representing all the people, had the muscle and perspective to succeed in this task. Thus was born state capitalism, able to industrialize nations at a forced pace and replace imports by converting itself into the major exporter. Its champions were Lázaro Cárdenas of Mexico, Juan Domingo Perón of Argentina, Eduardo Frei Montalva of Chile, Getulio Vargas of Brazil, Velasco Alvarado of Peru, and Fidel Castro of Cuba. A few, Frei Montalva among them, acted out of democratic principle. Others, such as Cárdenas, acted out of revolutionary nationalism. Still others, Perón and Vargas among them, were influenced by fascism, while some, such as Alvarado, were militarists. For his part, Castro was a Stalinist, convinced of the intrinsic virtues of collectivism and the administrative organization introduced by Lenin in the USSR. All agreed on one point: the economic solution for the Latin American people resided in a strong state that would guide them to a superior level of development and collective happiness.

That certainty fell to pieces at the end of the 20th century. After testing every experiment and seeing the continual failure of agrarian reforms and of nationalized business and natural resources (such as Mexican and Venezuelan petroleum and Chilean copper) with all the ensuing disasters of state capitalism — corruption, backwardness, and a rise in the cost of living — Latin Americans abandoned any illusion about conventional interpretations and accepted a devastating truth: at the end of the 20th century they were much poorer than their ancestors had been in relation to their neighbors Canada and the United States, ten times poorer if one compared the per capita incomes of both regions. If at the beginning of the 20th century the distance had been materially surmountable (the telephone, electricity, and the railroad were within the reach of all), by now the chasm of scientific progress in areas such as space research, biogenetics, atomic energy, cybernetics, and communications had reached epic proportions, shaping two substantially different worlds.

Are there any hopeful signs for Latin America? Indeed, the collapse of state capitalism and the discrediting of collectivism have restored to civil society, at least according to considerable public opinion, the central role it had lost. This has sparked a privatization of assets under state control. They have forsaken the Keynesian idea of using public spending to stimulate growth at the cost of large deficits. They have abandoned the inflationary practices of excessive indebtedness and incurring social expenses without first having the necessary tax funds. They have accepted globalization as a positive stance for the benefit of all, even though the period of adjustment may be painful due to the dismantling of the protectionist barriers maintaining certain costly, inefficient, and backward national industries. All these measures form part of the reformation of Latin governments into members of the modern global community, similar to the "convergence accords" struck by the European Union nations to unify their currencies, and to the economic policies preached by American and Canadian politicians.

More good news is the southern cone's emerging common market of 200 million people, Mercosur, with a per capita income of approximately $5,000 at the start of the 21st century, and its clear desire to be integrated into the commercial and technological networks of the First World. A similar desire drove Mexico to link its economic destiny to the U.S. and Canada. Also, in Central America, Costa Rica has ceased to be the democratic exception. For the first time in the region's turbulent history, there are no civil or inter-border wars, and its seven governments, including Panama's and Belize's (the predominantly black, English-speaking nation created by the British in the 19th century alongside Guatemala), are the product of free elections involving all political forces, even the guerilla groups of yesteryear now as leftist parties willing to accept democratic rules.

What caused such a dramatic shift? Clearly, the Cold War's end was a major factor, as were the obvious failure of the economic formulas taught throughout most of the 20th century. These two points seem to have convinced nearly all of the ruling classes that no valid alternatives exist to democracy and a free-market economy based on private property. The proof is in the turnaround made by traditionally statist parties, such as Argentina's Justicialism and Mexico's PRI defeated by the PAN in the 2000 elections after seven decades of hegemony. Less visible is an enthusiasm for this switch in paradigm. The shift has not taken place as the result of a real change of opinion based on informed analysis, but rather, as a result of the collapse of old political conceptions. Tinged with certain nostalgia for the glory days of revolution, the overall conclusion is that this path is not ideal, but the only viable route.

In any case, an analysis by those who are well educated is one thing and the perception of the masses is another. An earlier chapter began with a reference to the many societies, Venezuelan, Peruvian, Ecuadorian, and others that attacked their own democratic institutions. The cause was a progressive impoverishment created by inflation that consumed their buying power and precluded job opportunities. They may have never felt that the state in which their lives as citizens developed was organized for their advantage and enjoyment. They may have felt that it was more an alien entity run by individuals looking after their own interests. They may have never seen their government officials as true representatives. In their view, simply, the state was there for *others*. As a result, attempts to demolish it were met with applause and complacency. Rage and confusion are poor counselors.

8. Escape From The Labyrinth

The contents of this book so far provokes a final question. Despite its history, is it possible for Latin America to leave underdevelopment behind and reach the same levels of economic and scientific progress as the rest of the Western world in Europe, United States, Canada, and Australia? Yes, of course. Nations and cultures can, in fact, change. No fates are irrevocable. Those who know the histories of Japan, Singapore, Korea, and even Spain, know that it is entirely possible to make a full swing toward economic and cultural advancement.

What sorts of changes are needed, then, and how can they be implemented? The answer to this question can only be reached by closely examining the ideas and proposals that in our time have helped to rescue certain nations from abject poverty and consolidate the prosperity of others.

The Importance of Democracy

In 1989, the Berlin Wall was literally hammered to bits, and the states that formerly comprised the Eastern Bloc made a 180-degree political and economic turn. In Latin America, dictatorships fell one by one — with the exception of Cuba — and every nation, sooner or later, embraced the system of democracy to suit the new reality. They knew that democracy had no easy solution for their economic and social woes but for the first time clearly understood that its supreme value was rooted in a rational and peaceful method of conducting collective decision-making. As a system, democracy was good. The decisions, however, could be good, bad, or worse, depending on the quality and quantity of the information available to the electorate and its dominant values. The system itself, however, could not be dismissed. To say that democracy was not good for Latin Americans was like saying that arithmetic, peace, and rationality were incomprehensible to the human psyche. After all, the twenty most prosperous and stable societies on earth governed under a democratic system. For the first time in nearly two centuries of established Latin American republics, the majority valued the democratic process. Its immature confidence in governments run by strongmen and provincial *caudillos*, until then the norm in Latin America's authoritarian cultures, had been thoroughly shaken.

Furthermore, committed to preserve democratic systems, many nations today partner advantageously in diverse federations while expressly excluding from their international organizations all those who reject democratic methods. No state may belong to the European Union, the OAS, Mercosur, and — at least in the wording of the given agreements — the Andean Pact, the Río Group, or the Parlacén, if its government did not result from open and fair elections. No longer in vogue is the concept of a benevolent authoritarianism legitimizing figures such as Perón, Getulio Vargas, Velasco Alvarado, or Fidel Castro establishing social justice and collective happiness at bayonet point.

THE PRIMACY OF CIVIL SOCIETY

Let us explore another beneficial idea of our time, extracted from the experience of many decades of onerous waste, corruption, and economic failures. Privatization of public goods is now taking place in all latitudes, resulting from the belief, confirmed a thousand times by reality, that it is society and not the state that has the task of creating wealth. Business people fulfill the task more efficiently than bureaucrats since the results of such private management tend to be fairer and benefit the whole of society rather than, as Marxists have believed, just those who control the goods of production.

One by one, all modern states bloated and paralyzed by decades of statist practices, with better or worse results have proceeded to transfer most of the assets from their direct management to society's. This has happened in England and France, Spain and Argentina, Chile, Mexico, and Peru. Sometimes these privatizations have been made in a murky manner, along the way illegally enriching a number of persons who seem to fill the earlier role of "favorites" to the Crown. Other times, societies have succumbed to the fallacy of "natural monopolies," impeding healthy competition. But in every case, a net gain has resulted for the user of the privatized service or the buyer of the final product. In general, the user benefits from better goods and services, often at better prices, a fact that frees resources for more economic transactions.

THE SOVEREIGN CONSUMER

Citizens have achieved another way of appearing before society and before the state, something barely mentioned even a few years ago. Now it is the *consumer* who has and demands rights and wears a ubiquitous identity, for we are all constant consumers of something. A concept has emerged that has increased and dignified democracy — "consumer sovereignty." This concept describes a person who uses his money to select freely whatever satisfies him and does not willingly accept politicians or bureaucrats making his consumer decisions for him, however good their declared intentions. If there is one thing we know with total accuracy in this realistic era, it is that the psychological motivations of public servants or employees are the same as the rest of humanity. They pursue their own ends, desire power and prestige, tend to be less than careful with the goods of others — especially if their management is not audited continually — and have no higher altruistic impulse than ordinary folks.

Sovereign consumers understand that they can better exercise their rights in a free economy without hindrances or subsidies because any privilege assigned to a powerful person or group, or any obstacle introduced on behalf of a preferred person or community, ends up distorting the general system of prices and costs, raising the prices of products and services and affecting the whole of production. Sovereign consumers have discovered that artificial "corrections" intervening in the market are almost always more harmful than the ills they seek to alleviate. They know that the market is imperfect — people do not always make the best economic decisions — but they have learned that all-too-fallible politicians and bureaucrats cannot guess with any more success than the economic agents of civil society.

Neither do sovereign consumers fear, as occurred until recent years, admonitions that the market generates losses when left to its own devices. Much better educated than their predecessors, consumers today essentially know that certain incompetent producers tend to be punished by the market and may even vanish, taking with them the jobs they offer. They have learned that expending resources to maintain an inefficient operation destroys earnings and diverts capital that would be far more useful in other production areas, causing far greater damage than accepting that those not satisfying consumers be stamped out by the competition. This is not *economic Darwinism,* as it has been demagogically called, but pure common sense. It is what Joseph Schumpeter called *creative destruction,* a process that ensures the healthy existence of competitive tension. Without the risk of failure, the impetus to improve is very weak. Without competition, the machinery of progress becomes completely clogged, as does the will to innovate and create faster, more efficient, and more comfortable goods that help define what we call progress.

CONTROL OF PUBLIC AND BUREAUCRATIC SPENDING

Certainly, 21st century individuals, if well versed, understand far better than their predecessors how wealth is created and squandered. They also harbor few illusions regarding the intentions of politicians, having watched them do terrible things with the community's resources.

In extreme cases, they have seen politicians empower themselves with what belonged to society, what society had provided through taxes. They have seen them all too frequently employ those gains to buy supporters at election time, subsidize friends who finance political campaigns, and keep party members satisfied.

One of the great economists of the 20th century, James Buchanan, won a Nobel Prize precisely by demonstrating the economic impact of political decisions. Every public act has a cost, an obvious but oft forgotten truth. Since all public acts must be paid for and cost the public money, it is the public's responsibility to be vigilant, to watch for such expenditures, to propose measures that discourage waste (such as constitutional limits on debt), and to assure that capital is used for the community's actual benefit and not for supporters of the government of the moment. We must understand, exactly and correctly, the relationships of power. In rationally organized modern societies, politicians receive a *mandate* rather than *carte blanche*, and society must scrutinize the government and not the other way around, as has often happened.

Buchanan and his researchers have refined an old concept for the benefit of modern thought. We now accept, albeit sadly, that there is no such thing as an actual *common good*. There can be no acts of government that benefit all of us equally. The bridge that links two cities on opposite shores inevitably means that a school or hospital will not be built — for lack of resources. Moreover, today we understand that we dwell not in a community of altruistic archangels, but among human beings with good and bad instincts and attitudes, and conflicting interests. As we humbly accept our weaknesses, we should counter them by always promoting neutral and abstract measures beyond the grasp of the more powerful and influential and preserving an implacable system for controlling and auditing public acts. Herein lies possible equality. The false equality, imposed by the subjective generosity of others, almost always leads to injustice and insult.

No Sustained Development Without Institutions

What else has contemporary society learned at the end of the millennium? For one thing, *institutionalists* have established their prestige. Douglas North, also a Nobel laureate, carefully studied the histories of the most prosperous nations and found that the ones that guaranteed property rights — with clear laws and reasonably efficient courts — tended to repeat the process that led to the creation of wealth. In environments protected by states subject to the rule of law, people could work, save, and invest without fearing that arbitrary acts of government would deprive them of their accumulated wealth.

Such a legally secure environment was necessary to stimulate one of the most important qualities of creators of wealth: the impulse that leads them to restrict spending and postpone immediate gratification in exchange for the promise of attaining greater material compensation for themselves and their children in the future. This can only happen in states truly subject to the rule of law. It cannot take place in states where citizens are subject to unpredictable and capricious actions by enlightened and "irreplaceable" governments or "revolutionaries," persons persuaded that they know far better than the rest of humanity how to find happiness for others. Those who think themselves ethically superior to the society they live in merely prove themselves instead to be among the major creators of instability and poverty in recorded history. Why should anyone put off spending and consuming if he does not know whether tomorrow he will be deprived of his possessions? How can anyone plan for the long term — a decisive factor for development — if his existence is marked by fear of contingency?

It is no wonder that reasonable people living in states where the legal systems are insignificant send their capital to Switzerland, London, or Miami for security, depriving their own countries of indispensable resources. Such people seek out states subject to the rule of law and shelter from the sudden acts of revolutionaries or officials that place themselves above institutions. These acts are often carried out in the name of social justice, praised by revolutionaries but invariably leading to the redistribution of poverty among a growing number of desperate people.

THE ARROGANCE OF REVOLUTIONARIES

Who are these pathetic characters dedicated to "doing good" while achieving only the opposite? In other words, who are these revolutionaries? Austrian economist and jurist Hayek asked himself this same question, as did Edmund Burke before him. Hayek came to a conclusion that is today a conventional perception: these are the instigators who suffer from *fatal arrogance*. These individuals think they know — far better than the free market — what society should produce and what it should consume. They are convinced that they are enlightened by the gods and by their ideologies and must guide their fellow citizens to the Promised Land, even if it requires whips and dogs to do it, since no other way appears to move the flock toward an unasked-for destination.

Persons afflicted with this fatal arrogance invariably end up becoming the tormentors of their neighbors, incapable of understanding what people with a truly modern worldview see clearly: no social order is more than just that which spontaneously arises from the decisions of millions, each individual possessing some information that no one else can fully understand and that helps that individual attain his/her goals. These arrogant revolutionaries and enlightened *caudillos* do not understand the folly of trying to replace the prodigious process of change and creation in a spontaneous order with weak ideas born out of the good intentions of benevolent tyrants or groups mysteriously anointed by a savior ideology.

THE DANGER OF IDEOLOGIES

As Popper's conclusions reveal, ideologies can never be right because they stem from an original intellectual error: the presupposition that history is like an arrow shot in a certain direction at a measurable speed. Indeed, historicism entailed viewing the human plight as linear with a beginning, a middle, and an end, supposing, moreover, that ideologues, especially Marxist ideologues, knew beforehand the plot and its happy ending.

But is not the reasoning of Hayek, Popper, and Buchanan also an ideology? Do not some of their ideas form what the French call *la pensée unique*, "the only right way to look at things," that politically-correct straitjacket denounced by the enemies of "open society"? Actually, no. If we carefully observe the central ideas of modern thought, we see that they propose neither a final destination nor the ultimate social model, not only because they cannot predict them, but also because they deliberately do not suggest them. All that the most respected thinkers propose and promise is to provide the means of participation so that free, spontaneous societies can, through their own acts, define the present and glimpse the future they wish to explore. One will have advances and retreats in terms of prosperity and peace. History is open country, and it is exciting precisely because it is so unpredictable.

THE INDIVIDUAL'S RESPONSIBILITY TO HIS DESTINY

Naturally, there are those who say that the model of the free and open society is the model of the henhouse, and lifting an image from Aesop's wonderful fables they note that the fox wants freedom so that he may move around the henhouse unimpeded, stealing goods at will from the unfortunate who do not know how to defend their interests and need someone big to protect them. Fortunately, modern thought has annihilated that fallacy with incontestable experience. In Chile, the "AFP" — mutual investment funds for the employed — have functioned for over 15 years. Up to now, the accounts have provided an average yield of more than 11 percent annually, and their investors have accumulated an impressive savings surpassing $40 billion, securing for them a peaceful retirement.

In Chile (as in the U.S., where 60 million people own shares in the stock market), the market is no longer just for the foxes, but also for the hens. If there is any truly revolutionary entity on earth, it is not the Central Committee of some archaic communist party or other, but the electrifying stock market — with all of its nervous shouting — to which thousands of companies bring their imagination and innovations to invite us on their exciting economic adventures.

The revolution of the AFP — a Latin American institutional construction fundamentally conceived by José Píñera in Chile — finally put to rest pension funds designed for common distribution, in which wage earners, in the name of social justice, were divested of their earnings through two equally repugnant means: they were deprived of the legitimate interests they could aspire to in the market and their savings were devalued through inflation, caused by irresponsible management of currency. As a result wage earners, upon reaching retirement age when they most needed their savings, received meager pensions that barely covered living expenses. The Chilean experience taught citizens that there was nothing healthier than instilling a sense of individual and familial responsibility. Every adult should prepare for retirement. Experience has shown that leaving it to the state could be very dangerous and that no one safeguarded citizens' earnings better than themselves. The benefits of the astonishing vitality of capitalism could reach the greatest majority of people to make them stockholders and possessors of capital, a fact that without a doubt reduced labor conflicts, increased the ties that united society, and increased exponentially the savings available for collective development. In other words, from a practical point of view, a retirement system based on capitalization — on individual investment accounts — is infinitely superior to common distribution, or a social security system tinged falsely with the idea of solidarity. In the same way, also demolished was the superstition that the quality of a state could be measured by the public spending it incurred. On the contrary, now a successful state was measured by the economic model that best allowed the creation of wealth, so that social service spending would scarcely be needed because everyone or just about everyone able to work would be taking care of his or her own life without having to appeal to the sympathy of certain groups or public charities.

Recently, *Society* magazine, published by Transaction at Rutgers University, did the math to illustrate how savings benefit from long-term compound interest. For an average American college graduate who begins working at age 22 and retires at 65 and who earns an average professional salary throughout his life, saving 10 percent of the salary and investing it in the stock market should — if the market's average performance over the last 70 years continues — allow him to receive a check of almost $4 million, a more than sufficient amount to guarantee a splendid retirement and even an inheritance for family members.

THE FORMATION OF HUMAN CAPITAL

The aforementioned example contains one less-than-innocent proviso. The subject of our simple calculation is a "college graduate," an important stipulation. As Gary Becker, Nobel laureate, fully demonstrated in *The Economic Approach to Human Behavior*, human capital is a basic factor in the equation of economic success. A person's academic formation is fundamental. Equally vital are an individual's values, attitudes, and beliefs in facing the task of creating wealth for personal enjoyment and the community's benefit.

Classic economists generally cited capital, work, and land as the factors that, in different combinations, produced certain results. Rarely, however, did they add cultural factors to the balance when trying to explain the success or failure of a people. Today, thanks to the work of "culturalists" such as Becker and Harrison, we know that this elusive, vaporous, sometimes uncomfortable, and almost always "politically incorrect" element contains the key to understanding many failures and more than a few triumphs.

Today's heritage of modern thought easily proves the accuracy of the culturalist approaches. In Guatemala, as in all of Central America (but perhaps with greater vigor than in any other nation in the region), Evangelical Protestants have won over a segment of society that, according to some, comprises about 50 percent of the population. The penetration among the indigenous peoples is apparently much deeper, nevertheless occurring only in certain communities with others remaining Catholic. The contrast, for example, is very evident among the *Cachikeles*. Some of their communities have become Evangelical, while others have held on to Catholicism, mixed, as is customary there, with their ancestral pre-Columbian religious practices.

Estuardo Zapeta, a sociologist associated to the Francisco Marroquín University, and other social researchers have managed to observe several phenomena that recall the hypotheses Max Weber formulated at the beginning of the last century. The Evangelical *Cachikeles* are notably more prosperous than their Catholic counterparts. Is this, as Weber suggested, the result of Calvinist values? Not exactly. It is the consequence of basic cultural behaviors resulting from the conversion to a new and very demanding faith. Evangelical *Cachikeles* do not drink alcohol, a fact that makes them more responsible workers and enhances their capacity to save money. They seldom commit adultery, allowing for more stable families. They do not steal, and that generates more work opportunities since employers, even Catholic employers, appreciate this honesty in their workers. Furthermore, Evangelical *Cachikeles* can count on a church that serves as a general source of mutual support, giving them additional opportunities to overcome obstacles and improve their economic status. As those who have adopted a modern perspective well know, a people's economic success and social peace will be proportional to the quantity and quality of their human capital.

This last observation is crucial to understanding that a society must concentrate its efforts on improving human capital if it wants to gain a prominent place in the world. It must educate more and better, primarily during children's formative years, when character and certain behavioral habits and skills are first developed that will later allow for more complex cultural forms.

EDUCATION AND VALUES

If we teach our children to define and set goals, to be orderly, punctual, fair, respectful of authority, tolerant, responsible, intellectually curious; if we reward their efforts and teach them the value of a hierarchy based on merit; if we train them to vote, to make collective decisions in a peaceful way; and if we urge them to obey just laws and applaud their adherence to fair play, we increase our society's chances for greater collective wealth the moment these youngsters enter the working world. This is precisely what the culturalists have found.

This discovery contains a universal quality worth taking into consideration. As no one today denies, we live in a world that tends to standardize the goals of the dissimilar parts that compose it, necessarily tending to unify the means of reaching them. If the quality of life to which we aspire includes comfortable housing, efficient appliances, fast and secure transportation, appetizing and nutritious food, comfortable and clean cities with low crime rates and well-equipped sanitation systems, then we must create the wealth necessary to obtain these goods and services, wealth that can only be generated through the constant growth of production and yield.

GLOBALIZATION AS OPPORTUNITY

By now, it is an almost axiomatic point in modern thinking that it is crucial to enter fearlessly into globalization as much to attain these goals as to have the necessary tools, despite the warnings of some fortunetellers. For Latin America to get investment capital, it will have to look beyond its frontiers, and for know-how, wider markets for its goods, commercialization techniques, development models, and mechanisms to transfer and receive science and technology. No one should be embarrassed to seek in other countries the best way to attain these things, a fact brought home by Japan's astonishing trajectory since the middle of the 19th century. The Japanese were not the only people who learned how to benefit from globalization. In the century just ended, the

Germans sought in England the secrets of industrialization, and if today the United States has the world's best medical schools, it is because universities deliberately and unreservedly copied the German model of medical education.

It took medieval Europeans 500 years to produce paper in industrial quantities after slowly adopting a method developed by the Chinese and transferred by the Arabs. Yet, the Koreans took just 20 years to build automobiles and transport them to the opposite ends of the earth. Today, thanks to the examples of Taiwan, Singapore, Korea, and Hong Kong (despite their occasional slips into financial crisis), we know it is possible to go from poor to rich, from Third World to First, in a single generation. This leap is accomplished by opening nations to the world's great economic and scientific flow, opening economies to competition and collaboration, and accepting without shame the guidance of the great epicenters of civilization.

POLITICAL AND ECONOMIC FREEDOM

At the beginning of the third millennium, what is the cardinal idea behind modern thinking? It is the idea of freedom, along with confidence in the enormous advantages derived from an organization of power where authority, control, and initiative fundamentally rest in civil society. This freedom means the ability to produce, sell, and trade. It also includes the political freedom to create the right institutions and defend ourselves against the arrogant ideologues who presume to tell us how we should live our lives rather than letting us choose, without trampling on the rights of others, what we deem most useful and satisfying.

The just-concluded 20th century has been, in essence, a period of barbaric massacres and sinister dictatorships, but in the midst of that terrible landscape, some outstanding thinkers were able to search through the debris to find the seminal ideas that can carry societies into the new millennium. This intellectual inheritance must be safeguarded, built on and passed on to new generations. This is Latin America's most urgent task, and without a doubt, the way out of the labyrinth.

Bibliography

1. A Suspicious Origin: Fraud, Sophisms and Other Theological and Judicial Traps

AA.VV. *La ética en la conquista de América*. Consejo Superior de Investigaciones Científicas, Madrid, 1984.

Abellán, José Luis. *Historia crítica del pensamiento español*. (4 vol.). Espasa Calpe, Madrid, 1981.

Bataillon, M. y Saint-Lu, A. *El padre Las Casas y la defensa de los indios*. Ariel, Barcelona, 1974.

Castro, Américo. *Aspectos del vivir hispánico*. Cruz del Sur, Santiago de Chile, 1949.

Chaunu, Pierre. *Conquista y explotación de los nuevos mundos*. Labor, Barcelona, 1973.

Dawson, Christopher. *Los orígenes de Europa*. Ediciones Rialp, Madrid, 1991.

Fernández Herrero, Beatriz. *La utopía de América*. Anthropos, Barcelona, 1992.

Hanke, Lewis. *La lucha española por la justicia en la conquista de América*. Aguilar, Madrid, 1959.

Las Casas, Fray Bartolomé. *Brevísima relación de la destrucción de las Indias*. Fontamara, Barcelona, 1981.

León Portilla, M. *El reverso de la conquista*. Joaquín Mortiz, Barcelona, 1964.

Henríquez Ureña, Pedro. *Historia de la cultura en la América Hispánica*. Fondo de Cultura Económica, México, 1968.

Hernández Sánchez-Barba, Mario. *Historia de América*. (3 vol.). Alhambra, 1980.

Malmberg, Bertil. *La América hispanohablante*. Istmo, Madrid, 1992.

Menéndez Pidal, Ramón. *El padre Las Casas, su doble personalidad*. Espasa-Calpe, Madrid, 1981.

Morales Padrón, Francisco. *Historia general de América*. Espasa-Calpe, Madrid, 1962.

Mörner, Magnus. *La Corona española y los foráneos en los pueblos de indios en América*. Ediciones de Cultura Hispánica, Agencia Española de Cooperación Internacional, Madrid, 1999.

O'Gorman, Edmundo. *La invención de América*. Fondo de Cultura Económica, México, 1977.

Picón-Salas, Mariano. *De la Conquista a la Independencia*. Fondo de Cultura Económica, México, 1971.

Rodríguez Monegal, Emir. *Noticias secretas y públicas de América*. Tusquets, Barcelona, 1984.

Tovar, Antonio. *Lo medieval en la Conquista y otros ensayos americanos*. Seminario y Ediciones, Madrid, 1970.

Ullmann, Walter. *Historia del pensamiento político en la Edad Media*. Ariel, Barcelona, 1999.

Uslar Pietri, Arturo. *En busca del Nuevo Mundo*. Fondo de Cultura Económica, México, 1969.

Zavala, Silvio. *Ensayos sobre la colonización española en América*. Emecé, Buenos Aires, 1944.

Zea, Leopoldo. *América como conciencia*. Cuadernos Americanos, México, 1953.

2. ONE STATE TO THE DISSATISFACTION OF ALL

AA.VV. *Historia de la Inquisición en España y América*. (2 vols.). BAC. Madrid, 1984.

Albi, Julio. *La defensa de las Indias*. Instituto de Cooperación Iberoamericana. Ediciones Cultura Hispánica, Madrid, 1987.

Bamford Parkes, Henry. *La historia de México*. Editorial Diana, México, 1991.

Bennasar, Bartolomé. *Historia de los españoles*. (2 vols.). Editorial Crítica, Barcelona, 1989.

Cierva, Ricardo de la. *Historia total de España*. Editorial Fénix, Madrid, 1997.

Comella, Beatriz. *La inquisición española*. Ediciones Rialp. Madrid, 1999.

Fornés Bonavía, Leopoldo. *Fundamentos de Historia de América*. Editorial Playor, Madrid, 1986.

Gasca, Pedro de la. *Descripción del Perú (1553)*. Universidad Católica "Andrés Bello", Caracas, 1976.

Hidalgo Huerta. *España en Hispanoamérica*. Editorial Complutense, Madrid, 1998.

Iwasaki, Fernando. *Inquisiciones peruanas*. Renacimiento, Sevilla, 1997.

Jiménez Losantos, Federico. *Los nuestros: cien vidas en la historia de España*. Planeta, Barcelona, 1999.

Jones, Archer. *The Art of War in the Western World*. Barnes & Noble, New York, 1997.

Kamen, H. *Historia de la Inquisición en España*. Alianza Editorial, Madrid, 1985.

Keegan, John. *Historia de la guerra*. Planeta, Barcelona, 1995.

Kirkpatrick, F.A. *Los conquistadores españoles*. Ediciones Rialp, Madrid, 1999.

Laviana Cuetos, María Luisa. *La América española, 1492-1898*. Temas de Hoy/Historia 16, Madrid, 1996.

Lewin, Boleslao. *Los judíos bajo la Inquisición en Hispanoamérica*. Editorial Dédalo, Buenos Aires, 1960.

Lovett, A.W. *La España de los primeros Habsburgos (1517-1598)*. Labor, 1989.

Lunenfeld, Marvin. *Los corregidores de Isabel la Católica*. Labor, 1989.

Morner, Magnus. *Historia social latinoamericana*. Universidad Católica "Andrés Bello". Caracas, 1979.

Ots Capdequí, J.M. *El estado español en las Indias*. Fondo de Cultura Económica, México, 1982.

Parker, Geoffrey. *La revolución militar*. Editorial Crítica, Barcelona, 1990.

Partner, Peter. *God of Battles*. HarperCollins, London, 1997.

Rodríguez-Moñino Soriano, Rafael. *Razón de Estado y dogmatismo religioso en la España del XVII*. Editorial Labor, Barcelona, 1976.

3. BLACKS IN A PERSISTENTLY RACIST SOCIETY

Bowser, Frederick. *The African Slave in Colonial Perú: 1524-1650*. Standford University Press, California, 1974.

Curtin, Philip. *The Atlantic Slave Trade: A Census*. University of Wisconsin Press, Madison, 1969.

Fermoselle, Rafael. *Política y color en Cuba. La guerrita de 1912*. Editorial Colibrí. Madrid, 1998.

Franco, José Luciano. *Comercio clandestino de esclavos*. Editorial Ciencias Sociales, La Habana, 1980.

Lipschutz, Alejandro. *El problema racial en la conquista de América*. Siglo XXI, México, 1975.

Mannix, Daniel P. *Historia de la trata de negros*. Alianza Editorial, Madrid, 1970.

Marrero, Leví. *Cuba: economía y sociedad*. 15 vols. Editorial Playor, Madrid, 1978-1992.

Montaner, Carlos Alberto. *Viaje al corazón de Cuba*. Plaza & Janés, Barcelona, 1999.

Morner, Magnus. *Race and Class in Latin America*. Columbia University Press, New York, 1970.

Moreno Fraginals, Manuel. *El Ingenio*. 3 vols. Editorial Ciencias Sociales, La Habana, 1978.

Moya Pons, Frank. *Después de Colón*. Alianza Editorial, Madrid, 1986.

_____. *Historia contemporánea de la República Dominicana*. Fondo de Cultura Económica, México, 1999.

Novás Calvo, Lino. *Pedro Blanco, el negrero*. Espasa Calpe, Madrid, 1940.

Ortiz, Fernando. *Contrapunteo cubano del tabaco y del azucar*. Editorial Ariel, Barcelona, 1973.

_____. *Los negros esclavos*. Editorial Ciencias Sociales. La Habana, 1975.

Parcero Torre, Celia María. *La pérdida de La Habana y las reformas borbónicas en Cuba: 1760-1773*. Junta de Castilla y León, ívila, 1998.

Pérez-Cisneros, Enrique. *La abolición de la esclavitud en Cuba*. Litografía LIL, San José, Costa Rica, 1987.

Pérez de la Riva, Juan. *El barracón: esclavitud y capitalismo en Cuba*. Editorial Crítica, Barcelona, 1978.

Phillips, William D. *Historia de la esclavitud en España*. Editorial Playor, Madrid, 1990.

Rice, C. Duncan. *The Rise and Fall of Black Slavery*. Harper and Row, New York, 1975.

Rout, Leslie B., Jr. *The African Experience in Spanish America: 1502 to the present day*. Cambridge University Press, New York, 1976.

Saco, José Antonio. *Historia de la esclavitud de la raza africana en el Nuevo Mundo y en especial en los países Américo-hispanos*. 4 vols. La Habana, Cultura S.A., 1938.

Tannenbaum, Frank. *Slave and Citizen: the Negro in the Americas*. Alfred A. Knopf, New York, 1947.

Thomas, Hugh. *La trata de esclavos*. Planeta, Barcelona, 1997.

_____. *Cuba: The Pursuit of Freedom*. Harper and Row, New York, 1971.

4. Sex, Sexism, and Gender Roles

Acosta, José. *Historia natural y moral de las Indias*. Hispanoamérica de publicaciones, Sevilla, 1987.

Archibald, Zofia. *La Grecia antigua*. Editorial Óptima, Barcelona, 1997.

Ariès, Philippe y Béjin, André (Editores). *Western Sexuality*. Barnes & Noble, New York, 1985.

Braudel, Fernand. *El Mediterráneo*. Espasa Calpe, Madrid, 1989.

_____. *Bebidas y excitantes*. Alianza Editorial, Madrid, 1994.

_____. *A History of Civilization*. Penguin Books, New york, 1995.

Carcopino, Jerome. *La vida cotidiana en Roma en el apogeo del Imperio*. Ediciones Temas de Hoy, Madrid, 1993.

Casas de las, Bartolomé. *Historia de las Indias*. Fondo de Cultura Económica, México, 1951.

____. *Brevísima relación de la destrucción de las Indias*. Editora de los Amigos del Círculo de Bibliófilos, Madrid, 1981.

Cieza de León, Pedro. *La Crónica del Perú. Descubrimiento y Conquista del Perú*. Sankana, Buenos Aires, 1984.

Colón, Cristóbal. *Diario de a bordo*. Globus, Madrid, 1994.

Cortés, Hernán. *Cartas de la conquista de México*. Sarpe, Barcelona, 1985.

Díaz del Castillo, Bernal. *Historia verdadera de la conquista de la Nueva España*. Porrúa, México, 1968.

Deleito y Piñuela, José. *El desenfreno erótico*. Alianza Editorial. Madrid, 1995.

Hyam, R. *Empire and Sexuality*. University Press, Manchester, 1990.

Flacelière, Robert. *La vida cotidiana en Grecia en el siglo de Pericles*. Ediciones Temas de hoy, Madrid, 1989.

García-Merás, Emilio. *Pícaras Indias: historias de amor y erotismo de la Conquista. 2 vols.* Nuer Ediciones, Madrid, 1992.

Garcilaso, Inca. *Historia general del Perú. La Florida del inca*. Fondo de Cultura Económica, México, 1956.

Gautheron, Marie (Ed.). *El honor*. Ediciones Cátedra, Madrid, 1992.

Gordon, Richard. *A assustadora história do sexo*. Ediouro Publicaciones, S.A. Río de Janeiro, 1997.

Huizinga, J. *The Waning of the Middle Ages*. Arnold, London, 1924.

Keen, Benjamin. *La imagen azteca*. Fondo de Cultura Económica, México, 1971.

Madariaga, Salvador de. *Hernán Cortés: auge y ocaso del imperio español en América*. Espasa Calpe, Madrid, 1986.

Martínez Quiroga, J.L. *Historia de la galantería*. Gassó Editores, Barcelona, 1971.

Montanelli, Indro. *Historia de los griegos*. Globus, Madrid, 1994.

____. *Historia de Roma*. Globus, Madrid, 1994.

Morley, Sylvanus G. *La civilización maya*. Fondo de Cultura Económica. México, 1987.

Murphy, Emmett. *Historia de los grandes burdeles del mundo*. Ediciones Temas de Hoy, Madrid, 1989.

Núñez Cabeza de Vaca, Alvar. *Naufragios y comentarios*. Ediciones Orbis, Barcelona, España, 1982.

Pérez, Joseph. *Historia de España*. Crítica, Barcelona, 1999.

Pirenne, Jacques. *Civilizaciones antiguas*. Globus, Madrid, 1994.

Ruidíaz de Guzmán. *Anales del descubrimiento, conquista y población del Río de la Plata*. Historia 16, Madrid, 1986.

5. An Economy Twisted at Birth

Acton, Lord. *Ensayos sobre la libertad y el poder.* Unión Editorial, Madrid, 1999.

Baptista Gumucio, Mariano. *Latinoamericanos y norteamericanos.* Editorial Artística, La Paz, Bolivia, 1987.

Benegas Lynch, Alberto y Krause, Martín. *En defensa de los más necesitados.* Atlántida, Buenos Aires, 1998.

Burke, James y Ornstein, Robert. *The Axemaker's Gift.* G.P. Putnam's Sons, New York, 1995.

Cipolla, Carlo M. *Historia económica de la Europa preindustrial.* Alianza Editorial, Madrid, 1992.

Fukuyama, Francis. *Trust.* The Free Press, New York, 1995.

Grondona, Mariano. *Los pensadores de la libertad.* Editorial Sudamericana. Buenos Aires, 1989.

_____. *Las condiciones culturales del desarrollo económico.* Ariel-Planeta, Barcelona, 1999.

Hayek, Friedrich A. *Los fundamentos de la libertad.* Unión Editorial, Madrid, 1998.

Headrick R. Daniel. *Los instrumentos del imperio.* Alianza Editorial. Madrid, 1989.

Huberman, Leo. *História da riqueza do homen.* Livros Técnicos e Científicos Editora S.A. Río de Janeiro, 1986.

Jones, E.L. *Crecimiento recurrente: el cambio económico en la historia mundial.* Alianza Editorial, Madrid, 1998.

_____. *El milagro europeo.* Alianza Editorial, Madrid, 1990.

Jouvenel, Bertrand de. *Sobre el poder.* Unión Editorial. Madrid, 1998.

Landes, David S. *La riqueza y la pobreza de las naciones.* Vergara, Barcelona, 1999.

Maddison, Angus. *Historia del desarrollo capitalista. Sus fuerzas dinámicas.* Ariel, Barcelona, 1998.

Martínez Shaw, Carlos. *El Siglo de las Luces.* Temas de Hoy, Madrid, 1996.

Mendoza, Plinio A.; Vargas Llosa, ilvaro; Montaner, Carlos Alberto. *Manual del perfecto idiota latinoamericano.* Plaza & Janés, Barcelona, 1996.

_____. *Fabricantes de miseria.* Plaza & Janés, Barcelona, 1998.

North, Douglas C. *Estructura y cambio en la historia económica.* Alianza Editorial, Madrid, 1984.

Péronnet, Michel. *El siglo XVI: de los grandes descubrimientos a la Contrarreforma.* Akal, Madrid, 1990.

Reisman, George. *Capitalism.* Jameson Books, Ottawa, 1998.

Ribas, Armando. *Propiedad, fuente de libertad.* Fundación República para una Nueva Generación. Buenos Aires, 1997.

Rodríguez Braun, Carlos. *Estado contra mercado.* Taurus, Madrid, 2000.

_____. La cuestión colonial y la economía clásica. Alianza Editorial. Madrid, 1989.

Rothbard, Murray N. *Historia del pensamiento económico.* Unión Editorial, Madrid, 1999.

_____. *La ética de la libertad.* Unión Editorial. Madrid, 1995.

Sabino, Carlos A. *El fracaso del intervencionismo.* Editorial Panapo, Caracas, 1998.

Samhaber, Ernst. *Historia del comercio.* Zeus, Barcelona, 1963.

Schumpeter, Joseph A. *Historia del análisis económico.* Ariel, Barcelona, 1994.

Sédillot, René. *Historia de las colonizaciones.* Aymá S.A., Barcelona, 1961.

Simón Segura, Francisco. *Manual de historia económica mundial y de España.* Editorial Centro de Estudios Ramón Areces, S.A., Madrid, 1996.

Smith, Adam. *La riqueza de las naciones.* Edición de Carlos Rodríguez Braun. Alianza Editorial, Madrid, 1994.

Suárez, Luis. *Las grandes interpretaciones de la historia.* Ediciones Moretón, Bilbao, 1968.

Vásquez, Ian. *Global Fortune.* The Cato Institute, Washington, 2000.

Víctor Morgan, E. *Historia del dinero.* Ediciones Istmo, Madrid, 1972.

Voltes, Pedro. *Dos mil años de economía española.* Planeta, Barcelona, 1988.

Weber, Max. *Economía y sociedad.* Fondo de Cultura Económica, México, 1998.

_____. *Historia económica general.* Fondo de Cultura Económica. México, 1974.

6. 'LET OTHER PEOPLE DO THE INVENTING!'

A.A.V.V. *Historia de la educación en España y América.* Ediciones SM/Ediciones Morata, Madrid, 1992.

Abbagnano, N. y Visalberghi. *Historia de la pedagogía.* Fondo de Cultura Económica, México, 1964.

Abellán, José Luis. *Historia del pensamiento español: de Séneca a nuestros días.* Espasa, 1996.

Aguilar, Gaspar. *Expulsión de los moros de España.* Editorial Guadalmena, Sevilla, 1999.

Agustín, San. *Confesiones.* Alianza Editorial, Madrid, 1998.

Aurelio, Marco; Epicteto; Séneca. *Los estoicos.* Editorial Nueva Acrópolis, Madrid, 1997.

Bowen, James. *Historia de la educación occidental.* 3 vol. Editorial Herder, Barcelona, 1992.

Bravo Guerreira, Concepción. "Los incas" en *Historia de las Américas* (Tomo I). Alhambra Longman. Madrid, 1991.

Bury, John. *La idea del progreso.* Alianza Editorial, Madrid, 1971.

Bustamante Belaúnde, Luis. *La nueva universidad.* Universidad Peruana de Ciencias Aplicadas, Lima, 1998.

Cipolla, Carlo M. *Las máquinas del tiempo y de la guerra.* Crítica, Barcelona, 1999.

Díaz-Trechuelo Spínola, María Lourdes. "La cultura indiana en el siglo XVI" en *Historia de las Américas* (Tomo II). Alhambra Longman, Madrid, 1991.

_____. "*Cultura Indiana: plenitud de la Ilustración*" en *Historia de las Américas* (Tomo III). Alhambra Longman, Madrid, 1991.

Durant, Will. *Historia de la filosofía.* Diana, México, 1978.

Escalante Gonzalbo, Pablo. "Los aztecas" en *Historia de las Américas* (Tomo I). Alhambra Longman, 1991.

Fusi, Juan Pablo. *España: la evolución de la identidad nacional.* Temas de hoy, Madrid, 2000.

Garin, Eugenio. *La educación en Europa 1400-1600.* Crítica, Barcelona, 1987.

Guillermou, Alain. *Los jesuitas.* Oikos-tau. Barcelona, 1970.

Herlihy, David (ed.). *Medieval Culture and Society.* Harper Torchbooks, New York, 1968.

Letson, Douglas y Higgins, Michael. *The Jesuit Mystique.* HarperCollins, London, 1995.

López de Juan, Crescente y Plácido, Domingo. *Momentos estelares del mundo antiguo.* Ediciones Clásicas, Madrid, 1998.

López Piñero, J.M., Navarro, V. y Portela, E. *La revolución científica.* Historia 16. Madrid, 1989.

Montaner, Carlos Alberto. *No perdamos también el siglo XXI.* Plaza & Janés, Barcelona, 1997.

Mumford, Lewis. *Técnica y civilización.* Alianza Editorial. Madrid, 1998.

Sánchez Marín, José A. y López Muñoz, Manuel (Ed.) *Humanismo renacentista y mundo clásico.* Ediciones Clásicas, Madrid, 1991.

Sarrailh, Jean. *La España Ilustrada de la segunda mitad del siglo XVIII.* Fondo de Cultura Económica, México, 1992.

Strauss, Leo y Cropsey, Joseph (ed.) *Historia de la filosofía política.* Fondo de Cultura Económica, México, 1993.

Vernet, Juan. *Lo que Europa debe al Islam de España.* El Acantilado, Barcelona, 1999.

Vidal, César. *El legado del cristianismo en la cultura occidental.* Espasa Calpe, Madrid, 2000.

7. CAUDILLOS, MONTONEROS, GUERRILLAS, AND LIBERALS AND CONSERVATIVES

Arciniegas, Germán. *Biografía del Caribe.* Plaza & Janés, Bogotá, 1984.

Bibliography

Belaúnde, Víctor Andrés. *Bolívar y el pensamiento político de la revolución hispanoamericana.* Ediciones de la Presidencia de la República de Venezuela, Caracas, 1974.

Boulton, Alfredo. *El arquetipo iconográfico de Bolívar.* Ediciones Macanao, Caracas, 1984.

Freyre, Gilberto. *New World in the Tropics.* Alfred A. Knopf, New York, 1959.

Hanke, Lewis. *América Latina: Continente en fermentación.* Aguilar, México, 1961.

Herrera, Luis Alberto de. *La revolución francesa y Sudamérica.* Edición de la Cámara de Representantes del Uruguay, Montevideo, 1988.

Hobsbawn, E.J. *Nations and Nationalism since 1780.* Cambridge University Press, New York, 1990.

Kamen, Henry. *Nacimiento y desarrollo de la tolerancia en la Europa moderna.* Alianza Editorial, Madrid, 1967.

Krauze, Enrique. *Siglo de caudillos.* Tusquets Editores. Barcelona, 1994.

_____. *Biografía del Poder. Porfirio Díaz: Místico de la autoridad.* Fondo de Cultura Económica, México, 1991.

_____. *Biografía del Poder. Francisco I. Madero. Místico de la libertad.* Fondo de Cultura Económica. México, 1987.

Levaggi, Abelardo. "Las constituciones iberoamericanas en el siglo XIX" en *Historia de las Américas,* Tomo IV. Alhambra Longman, Madrid, 1991.

Lytle Schurz, William. *Latin America: a Descriptive Survey.* E.P. Dutton, New York, 1964.

Marichal, Juan. *Cuatro fases en la historia intelectual latinoamericana.* Fundación Juan March/Cátedra, Madrid, 1978.

Martínez Díaz, Nelson. *La independencia hispanoamericana.* Historia 16. Madrid, 1989.

Montaner, Carlos Alberto. *200 años de gringos.* Editorial Sedmay, Madrid, 1976.

Muñoz, Rafael F. *Santa Anna: el dictador resplandeciente.* Fondo de Cultura Económica, México, 1983.

Porter, Charles O. y Alexander J. Robert. *The Struggle for Democracy in Latin America.* The Macmillan Co., New York, 1961.

Ruiz Rivera, Julián B. "La independencia de los Estados Unidos: la forja de la nación norteamericana, 1763-1789" en *Historia de las Américas,* Tomo III. Alhambra Longman, Madrid, 1991.

Sánchez Agesta, Luis. *La democracia en Hispanoamérica.* Ediciones Rialp, Madrid, 1987.

Torre, Armando de la. *100 obras 1000 años.* Universidad Francisco Marroquín. Guatemala, 2000.

Trend, J.B. *Bolívar and the Independence of South America.* The Macmillan Co., London, 1948.

Vallenilla Lanz, Laureano. *Cesarismo democrático.* Caracas, 1919.

INDEX

Printed in the United States
70772LV00007B/95